LIVING TRUE

Lesbian Women Share Stories of Faith

LIVING TRUE

Lesbian Women Share Stories of Faith

Margaret O'Gorman and Anne Peper Perkins

PenUltimate Press, Inc.
Saint Louis, Missouri

Early praise for *Living True*

This is a wonderful, overwhelmingly positive collection of the stories about the spiritual journeys of lesbian Catholics told in their own voices. Like many other such anthologies, this contains some horrific tales of rejection falsely made in the name of God that are painful to read. They make clear the courage it takes to refuse to stay in abusive situations and poisonous environments, even when it means leaving home. It takes strength to search for spiritual nourishment elsewhere. Tragically, this is a well-trodden path for many. And yet, this collection also contains a surprising number of narratives that give voice to the experience of lesbian women finding among God's people in local Catholic parishes a spiritually enriching, supportive community. Their stories make evident the power of such embrace. For some, these experiences of church have enabled reconciliation with their parents, and most remarkable of all, strengthened the capacity of these women and the friends and family, even as they abide within it, lovingly to bear witness against hurtful official church teachings about diverse sexual identities and relationships. This book honors the spiritual journeys of those who stay in, as well as those who leave the church. One after the other joyfully testifies to God's steady invitation out of the closet. These women are giving birth with their very lives to a genuinely inclusive church. As the title indicates, they are indeed Living True to God's call.

> Patricia Beattie Jung
> Professor of Christian Ethics and Oubri A. Poppele
> Professor of Health and Welfare Ministries
> Saint Paul School of Theology
> Kansas City, Missouri

Living True uniquely portrays the complicated faith journey of twenty-one lesbian Catholic women to those not already sharing faith with them. These stories are all multifaceted but emphasize five themes: awakening, healing, trusting, appreciating, and celebrating. Hearing these women speak for themselves enables the reader to begin to absorb the pain, struggle, joy, and the enormous personal work these women have done just to become who they are. We witness their deep love for others and their confidence in God's love for them and theirs for God in a tradition that is deeply conflicted within itself about the diverse identities, orientations, and ways of loving within this community of faith. These women have had to work even harder than other women to find a healthy way of being Catholic, of living and loving, of ministering within this community, and contributing to it. Their stories reveal most lucidly the need for gender equality and gender justice because they suffer the most from its absence in church and society.

These stories moved me deeply because of the generosity of these women who have sufficiently overcome layers of internal and external prejudice and threats to their well-being to disclose their stories to us so we might be encouraged in our own journeys to "live true" and to change our attitudes and behaviors that continue to make this such a difficult journey in our unrepentantly misogynist church. These women are the survivors and thrivers who have matured, developed, and become comfortable with who they are. They allow us to appreciate their maturity, their generativity, and their lesbian integration as deeply spiritual women, not all of whom could do so and remain within the church. Those who have remained or returned to this faith community are truly exceptional and call the rest of us to become a more welcoming and hospitable community.

This volume will most immediately open fresh possibilities for Catholic lesbian women who have long needed such an inspiring collection of narratives of faith to offer inspiration, hope, and guidance along this journey and to reduce the fear and loneliness many still feel. These stories will also help spiritual directors work more deeply and broadly with their bisexual or lesbian directees and help therapists appreciate the depth of faith and spirituality that are a deep resource for these women and impel some to stay in the church and contribute to it. It will also offer fresh insights for ministry to gays and lesbians within the Catholic community as well as challenge both the behavior and public rhetoric of the church.

Janet K. Ruffing, RSM
Professor of the Practice of Spirituality and
Ministerial Leadership
Yale Divinity School
New Haven, Connecticut

Living True is an inspiring collection of personal stories told by lesbian women, describing in their own voices their struggles and eventual triumph to retain and nourish their faith within a church institution that denigrates their existence. From "Awakening" to "Celebrating," these strong, faith-filled women describe their journeys from despair and confusion to exploring diverse religious traditions and pastoral communities and, for some, to finding a Catholic spiritual home in which to live her faith and also both give and receive pastoral support within that community.

Amity P. Buxton, PhD
Founder, Straight Spouse Network and author,
*Unseen-Unheard: Straight Spouses from Trauma
to Transformation*

Publisher: PenUltimate Press, Inc.
Design/Production: Rose Design, Inc.
Printer: Publishers' Graphics
Cover Illustration: Unity, Monica Stewart

PenUltimate Press, Inc.
6900 Delmar Boulevard
Saint Louis, Missouri 63130
Phone: (314) 447-3888
E-mail: penultim@swbell.net
Web: www.penultimatepress.blogspot.com

Library of Congress Control Number: 2013914108

O'Gorman, Margaret 1946 –
Perkins, Anne Peper 1939 –

Living True: Lesbian Women Share Stories of Faith
184p.; 22.86 cm.
ISBN 13: 978-0-97606-75-9-7
Religion: Spirituality
Social Science: Lesbian Studies

Printed in the United States
Printing 10 9 8 7 6 5 4 3 2

Financial assistance for this project has been provided by the Missouri Arts Council, a state agency.

Dedication

I dedicate this book to Mary Tobias Hagan, CSJ, sister, mentor, friend.

Margaret O'Gorman

I dedicate this book to my beloved spouse Mary Sale and to the blessed memory of my parents, Ethel and Christian Peper.

Anne Peper Perkins

Acknowledgments

We are eager to thank so many, both individually and together:

I, Marge, want to thank Anne for being with me to the end: she has been encouraging and enthusiastic and affirming; we have laughed together; she has been a companion, offering understanding, wonderful comments, edits, and suggestions.

I, Anne, give loving thanks to Marge: for her enormous dedication in bringing our group together in the beginning, as well as for loving all of us contributors all the way through; for her creative and conscientious fine-tuning of her own short essays; for her constant graciousness towards me.

We both gratefully acknowledge our publisher, Winnie Sullivan, for her many kind suggestions in the pursuit of making this not just an important but a beautiful book—and for the fun we had in doing just that. We also want to thank her wonderful staff: senior editor, Judith Roos, and the graphic designers at Rose Design. Thanks as well to Mary Ellen Havard, who helped us to find Winnie in the first place, and to our endorsers who were so kind to take the time to read our manuscript and to lend their name to our efforts.

We are grateful to Sharon McMullen Orlet, who helped and encouraged Marge to gather together a core group. And thanks also to Kevin Minder, who gave Marge the idea of creating a narrative-container to hold together the stories. We are both so grateful to Jane Levdansky and Joan Lafferty who invited us into their home and shared their friends, many of whom became our faithful authors. We also acknowledge all those who showed interest in our book, especially those who had a story to tell even though they were unable to share it—and yet did share their own growth and excitement.

Again, as individuals:

I, Marge, wish to acknowledge the following: Mary Ellen and Casey Lopata, who helped us find our out-of-town authors, and my small church community—Wade Baughman, Tim Brennan, Carmela Garza, Jeff Goldone, Leo Berhorst, and Chris Wilkerson—for their insights, faith sharing, and the new lens they have given me to use as I read, reflect on, and pray with scripture. I am grateful to Michael Stancil for his faithful support and his commitment to our gay and lesbian community. I thank my family, and in particular, my brother and sister-in-law, Bob and Elaine O'Gorman, who have supported everything I have been involved with over the years. I am so grateful for my congregation, Franciscan Sisters of Mary, especially my leadership team, who supported and guided me and who have been my sisters through all these years.

I, Anne, want to thank my art-history-professor son Jonathan, who found the wonderful Harunobu print and the Roman fresco that illustrate the Appreciating and Healing sections. I also gratefully acknowledge the constant support and love of my entire extended family and that of my many dear friends and my eager church community—with particular gratitude to Delores Blount, who gave me special encouragement. Above all, I give my most profound thanks to my beloved spouse Mary Sale, for her daily acts of love and her eager interest in all that I do, including this project!

Deo Gratias.

LIVING TRUE

Lesbian Women Share Stories of Faith

Contents

Introduction

I am a woman religious, and I have been involved in lesbian, gay, bisexual, and transgendered (LGBT) ministry for more than ten years. I have been drawn to this ministry because of my concern for what many of my lesbian friends experience. In casual conversations and in pastoral settings I hear stories from women I care about regarding their struggle to come out, first of all to themselves and then to those close to them—family and friends, coworkers and acquaintances. Often this involves a struggle to fit in and to seem "normal." They tell me they even try to change themselves. But, they add, they do this only by doing a great disservice to themselves. In trying to change, they deny who they truly are.

My lesbian friends teach me that we don't consciously choose the people to whom we are attracted. Having lesbian friends in my life has helped me to have a personal interest in this ministry. These women lead me to see acceptance and inclusion as a justice issue.

I love the people I meet in this ministry—I find them interesting, talented, creative, zany, and fascinating. My desire to be involved in making our Catholic parishes more welcoming places for gay and lesbian Catholics grows as I find myself more and more immersed in this ministry.

The vision for this book began a number of years ago. For more than twelve years I have been reading about homosexuality within the context of the church. Most books are "about" our LGBT community. These works are mostly about gay men. I want to hear women speak for themselves and to let you, the reader—whether gay or straight—get to know them. I want to stop treating my lesbian sisters like something to be studied, to take them out from under the microscope where the straight community often looks at them as specimens and objectifies them. I want to catch the attention of the straight community and ask its members to listen to my lesbian sisters as they speak about their lives. Listen so that they can "be heard into speech," to borrow a phrase that was first used by theologian Nelle Morton when she talked about breaking out of silence into speech and being supported by those who truly hear what is most sacred to the soul.

I have been deeply touched by the stories and the lives of the women I have met over the years. I have experienced goodness and inclusion and generosity of spirit from the women in our lesbian community. I want others to see this and experience it for themselves.

I invite you into their lives to see the beauty, the pain and the struggle, the accomplishments, the growth and affirmation, the resolution of issues, the confidence and deep inner strength that is there. The intensity of their love and friendship, the gifts they have to offer the church, our society, and to you as well.

This book is about creating safe places for those who are giving voice and for those who are listening. It is a book about being welcoming and being welcomed. It is about telling stories to heal and to create change, about speaking up and out about inner longings and desires, dreams, hopes, and identities. It is about helping a new generation of Catholic women feel more at home.

It is a pastoral book, giving pastoral care and response to lesbian Catholic women. It is affirming the goodness and blessing of the lives of these women. It is helping the wider church to see the witness of these lives. It focuses on personal experience. It is part of a wider effort toward creating a world that embraces just love and just sexual ethics. It is about finding freedom in sexuality and being able to talk about it. It is about being more welcoming and more intentional in extending welcome. It is about helping our church change— one person in the pew at a time. It is about breaking down barriers.

It is a book of stories. Not just coming-out stories, although there are a number of them included in the following pages, but stories about spirituality: how lesbian and bisexual women find faith and live it; how God guides our lives; how we find our identity; and how much we contribute as couples, family, neighbors, and members of our parishes. It is about what makes our lives, our faith, and our spirituality flourish. It is about how we nourish our spirituality and how our faith community helps us on our journey.

As the women were writing their stories, I began writing some narrative pieces of my own. I wanted to journal about what was happening to our group as we met to discuss and share what we were writing. I wanted to capture the moments so I could savor them and honor them. I also found myself reflecting on who we were as a group and how we fit into our larger faith community.

I invite you to travel with me through these pages as I share my recollections and reflections with you at the beginning and end of each section. Travel with me as I introduce you to the women and the journey we took together through the months and years of sharing our stories and breaking open our lives to one another.

I welcome, you, the reader, to engage with us on this journey and to witness the lives of our women within these pages.

Margaret O'Gorman

I was among the original group of lesbian and bisexual women who gathered in January of 2008. Sister Marge saw a great need to have a book embracing lesbian spirituality within the Roman Catholic tradition. She enlisted the aid of a member of our parish, Sharon Orlet, a social worker and hospital chaplain who had offered to help facilitate the group. All of us who met that day in one way or another were associated with the church: some had been raised Catholic or had converted to Catholicism, and remained Catholic; others had found alternative religious homes; still others were no longer active in any formal religion. But all had been Roman Catholic at some time in their lives.

From the beginning, it was a gathering of earnest and loving and articulate women. There were about twenty women in the group, ranging in age from the thirties through the sixties. Some of us had been women religious, a number of us had had the same partner for many years, several of us had children and even grandchildren, a few had been in heterosexual marriages. Some of us came with our partners, and it was lovely to see the interactions between the couples as they talked of how they had met and how their relationship supported their spiritual lives. Many of us came alone, but very frequently had our own happy tales of intimate partners. A number of us had been or were still connected with a parish known for its openness and its commitment to social justice in our large Midwestern city.

We met every month or so, often at the house of a long-committed lesbian couple named Jane Levdansky and Joan Lafferty, and began to know one another better. Marge and Sharon asked us to begin writing our stories and suggested that we bring our first drafts to the group for encouragement and helpful criticism. We were given a number of questions to use as a starting point, questions like " How is my spirituality flourishing?" and "Who helps me on my journey?" There was a good deal of laughter—and some tears—and an increasing sense of closeness in the group.

Within nine months of our first meeting, after only about a half of the women in our group had come up with their stories, Sister Marge decided to reach out to women in other cities. She had worked in the LGBT ministry long enough to have a number of contacts she could call on. We were both delighted that her efforts succeeded in bringing in another thirteen stories via e-mail.

I am a former English-composition teacher, and so I offered to look at the stories as they came in to Marge, to do what I called "light editing." Mostly I corrected obvious grammar or punctuation errors, but I also tried to be aware of what could be expanded (or contracted) in the stories. And I asked for further clarification or modification if some portion of the piece seemed unclear or stylistically awkward.

The process for each piece was different. Very rarely a story could stand as written. Usually I would make at least minor suggestions, send the piece back with my annotations, and wait for the author to either agree or disagree and send her story back to me. The variety of their voices was always fascinating to me, and I worked hard never to interfere with what I heard as the voice of an individual writer. The light editing took place over a period of about three years. All through the process I particularly enjoyed the breadth of the shared experiences. And I slowly came to understand the whole subject of lesbian spirituality much more personally and more fully than ever before.

Once all the stories were in, including the final versions of those needing revisions, Marge and I met in the early Fall of 2011. Marge had written a number of short essays in order to bind together the stories, and so we inserted those after dividing the stories thematically. Once we had come up with a kind of structure, we started looking for a publisher. I talked to my dear friend Mary Ellen Havard, whose book *Breast Cancer: Four Seasons, Two Women, One Illness* had been published several years before by PenUltimate Press, a small nonprofit literary press in St. Louis, Missouri. When I asked if she thought her publisher, Winnie Sullivan, might be interested in our book, Mary Ellen offered to speak to her. Winnie was indeed interested and requested a letter of description and a sample of some of the stories as well as Marge's short essays. By November Marge and I heard that Winnie had agreed to publish our book. We were so grateful that we had found a publisher with almost miraculous speed.

Nine months later, we signed a contract with PenUltimate Press as the co-editors, and also sent out contracts to our contributors, henceforth to be known as "anthologists." Marge received the signed contracts back from all of the women, usually accompanied by both excitement and delight.

And after that came some of the most enjoyable and creative parts of the whole project!

Marge and I first met with Winnie on a regular basis starting in October of 2012. She gave us several tasks to accomplish, the first one being to find a new structure for the stories. Instead of using themes as an organizing factor, we came up with five sections reflecting five emotional states. Winnie also asked Marge to see how her short essays could fit in with this new structure. With my occasional suggestions and Winnie's encouragement, Marge worked for many weeks on her essays so that they could reflect both the general atmosphere of our meetings and the emotional and spiritual content of the stories themselves.

In the meantime I was given the much less onerous job of finding quotes for each section, and I decided to limit myself to women's writings. I found myself delighting in reading through many poems of Mary Oliver and Emily Dickinson and, of course, surfing the Internet as well for individual quotes. We were also discussing how the book should be illustrated, and I brought in to one of our meetings a lovely Indian miniature of mine showing two women seated very close and gazing at one another. We decided to look for other images of women couples from many parts of the world in order to suggest the universal nature of our book on spirituality.

Another question was what to name the book: after much discussion we agreed upon Winnie's suggestion, *Living True: Lesbian Women Share Stories of Faith*. About this time we adopted Marge's new titles for our five sections: Awakening, Healing, Trusting, Appreciating, and Celebrating.

An important task was to make a list of those who might review our book. Marge had met a number of people who had worked with the gay/lesbian community and offered to write to them. Winnie wrote to others who had similar background but whom Marge did not know personally. I simply picked some of my favorite writers and wrote asking them if they would be willing to read our manuscript. In mid-February I was fortunate enough to discover three books by Carol Lynn Pearson, a woman who has written numerous books of poetry and several plays, and also some nonfiction—all of them centering on the connection between Mormonism and the gay community. I wrote an e-mail to her and received a positive response on the same day! And slowly but surely, other reviewers and potential endorsers wrote back to us with positive answers.

The final creative part was putting the images and appropriate quotes at the beginning of each section, and finding an appropriate image for the cover of the book. Judith Roos, an editor at PenUltimate, had already been invaluable in researching and getting permissions for the quotes and images we wanted to use, and she is the one who found the image that graces the cover of our book, Monica Stewart's beautiful painting titled *Unity*.

Throughout this process Marge and I were moved by Winnie's gracious willingness to have us be so great a part in many of the more creative aspects of publishing our book. Unfailingly our meetings were marked by great courtesy and flexibility—and pleasure in each other's company.

It is my fervent hope that the stories in this book will bring solace—as well as challenge—to those who read them, no matter what their religious preference, sexual orientation, or gender. These are stories of love and fear and joy and gratitude and yearning to belong. And above all, these are stories of great spiritual courage.

I feel very blessed to have helped bring this book to birth.

Anne Peper Perkins

You Know My Voice

Lord, you are my shepherd, the one who knows my voice, recognizes me, and calls
        me by name.

You gather me up, hold me close, and feed me.

You strengthen me when I am weak, heal me when I am sick, and bind up all
        my wounds.

Lord, you are my shepherd, the one who refreshes my soul, invites me to the
        table, and welcomes me to dwell in your house.

I am your homosexual child, baptized into your flock, O Lord.

My family and I cry out to you for shepherds here on earth who, like you, know us,
        feed us, care for us, and invite us to your table.

        Amen.

Marie Lynette Aldapa
Ministry with Lesbian and Gay Catholics
Archdiocese of Los Angeles

My Faith Journey

Marie Lynette Aldapa

Marie Lynette Aldapa is a lifelong learner and an educator since 1986. The devoted daughter of Robert and Carolyn, she is also the loving godmother of Celeste and Jose. She is an enthusiastic teacher of many. An admirer of those who work for social justice, she aligns herself with agents of change. Lynette is a child of God, working on becoming an adult of God.

This prayer was a turning point for me in my faith journey. Our ministry, the Ministry with Lesbian and Gay Catholics in the Archdiocese of Los Angeles, was hurt by the stance the bishops of California took on Proposition 22, which preceded Proposition 8, the ban on same-sex marriages. On a personal level, I was not feeling loved, supported, or pastorally cared for by our church with such a stance. I was questioning why I was part of a church that does not allow me all seven sacraments—no sacrament of marriage (and no children of my own), no holy orders (when I was a child I thought nuns were given the female version of this sacrament). I knew that I had not chosen to be lesbian; however, I knew that I had chosen to remain Catholic. But now I felt like the church was saying publicly that I was unlovable…no marriage…no children…no family of my own…only a loveless life for me, devoid of any human embrace.

How I Came Up with This Prayer

On my way to the ministry's leadership meeting in which we were going to discuss what to do regarding Proposition 22, I was having a terrible crisis of faith. I felt so bad that, while driving in the rain on the freeways of Los Angeles, I actually thought about running my car off the road and preventing what seemed like a bleak future. I couldn't do it, of course, because it would hurt my parents (and besides, who would take care of my cat?). So, I would like to say that I raised my voice *to* God, but I actually raised my voice *at* God, yelling that I needed a sign…I needed to know that I was enduring this experience for a reason!

When I arrived, I was one of two lesbians at the leadership meeting. I was again a minority among minorities and feeling that my voice was one that would not be readily heard or understood. Yet I was chosen to lead us in the opening prayer. I was also asked, as one of the lesbians, to help write our ministry's response to Proposition 22, our ministry's prayer! My sign…my voice was heard…I was here for a reason…to give voice to the voiceless through this prayer.

I believed that the bishops, the shepherds of our church, were not shepherding their whole flock and were leaving some of the sheep vulnerable to the wolves. So my approach to writing the prayer was to refer to each biblical reference regarding shepherds. I prayerfully synthesized the essence of these verses and applied them to our situation. I bypassed the shepherds here on earth and lifted our voices directly to King David's Good Shepherd. This prayer is the result. This prayer is an answer to my prayer.

How We Pray It

This prayer is our official ministry prayer. We introduced it in a special rededication of the ministry Mass. It has been well received by laity and clergy alike. We use it at our various meetings, retreats, and special events. It is printed on cards that we hand out with our ministry's information. I personally pray it and know that it is a gift from God.

AWAKENING

Not knowing when dawn will come, I open every door.
— Emily Dickinson

Recollections...

Gathering Women Together

In gathering the stories, we begin by gathering women together. I had talked with a woman from our parish, Sharon McMillan Orlet, about my dream of putting together this book. She is a trained facilitator and had been involved in a woman's project similar to this one. She suggested that we call together a core group to plan and coordinate the project. I call Jane Levdansky and Joan Lafferty, whom I know to be leaders in our lesbian community, and ask them to host the meetings in their house. I have a list of lesbian women I know. Jane and Joan give me a list of their friends and acquaintances. Together, the four of us write a letter inviting forty women to the first meeting; twenty-two come.

Sunday, January 6, 2008

Jane and Joan still have their Christmas tree in their living room window. We sit around on their sofa and in cushy chairs. Women start coming in, and we go to the dining room and bring in a few more chairs. Still not enough as other women keep coming through the door. We scrounge around for more chairs and are pleased when we find a few folding chairs. We rearrange the circle we are sitting in because the circle keeps expanding to hold more women, all with stories to share. We are spread out, having moved from a circle to an oval, which now extends from the living room well into the dining room.

Since it is the feast of the Epiphany, I open our gathering by paraphrasing today's gospel:

"They saw a star and watched it until it stopped over the place where they were. When they saw that the star had stopped, they were overwhelmed with joy. They opened their treasures." I say, "This is the place where the star has stopped. It is time for us now to open our treasures." And I add, "You have not been just following the star—you, each of you, is a star. We are beginning this amazing writing project together: I invite you to reveal the beauty of your spirits, the strength of your souls, and the wonder of who you are."

We move from prayer to excited talking about being here. Some women express surprise at being asked to be at this meeting. Cathy says, "I am not out even to my family. How did you know I was lesbian?" Charlotte tells us, "It was a big risk to come here. I am not used to being around lesbians. I don't talk about my orientation in public." Margaret, on the other hand, says, "I was so excited about getting this letter!" She holds it up and waves it at us, "I wanted to frame it. It is exciting to be here and meet freely with other

Catholic women claiming their orientation." Theresa adds, "I put it on my desk so I could see it each day. I have thought about this everyday since then. I couldn't wait to be here with all of you."

Sharon leads us in discussing what this is all about. "We'd like you to write a story of your spirit—giving voice to your life and offering it to others. We have some questions for you to reflect on as you put your pens to paper."

More excitement circles the room. Questions arise; pieces of stories float around in the air as women tell parts of their stories, especially talking about coming out and coming to freedom. Joy fills the air, and a few giggles. Someone from over by the window says, "After we publish our book we can all be on *Oprah* together," and the room explodes with laughter.

———————————

Our next meeting at Joan and Jane's house was a month later, in February, on another pleasant Sunday afternoon.

The living room looks empty and less festive now that the Christmas decorations have been taken down and put away. We open this meeting by talking about Colleen, a friend of many of the women in the room. Colleen had died since our first meeting—suddenly, at the age of thirty-two—and her funeral had been the week before. We are all in shock because of this. She had been sick. She was hospitalized. Then she was on life support. Then she was dead. All within about ten days.

Colleen's story is our first story to share. As part of a brief prayer service, I tell a bit of what I know about Colleen and Mary as a couple: I recall that Colleen and Mary had grown up in the same city, in strict Catholic families. In grade school they become best friends. Colleen's family moved, but the girls keep in touch, sharing their friendship long distance as teenagers. Both of them stay involved in their parishes in high school and at the Newman Center through college. After finishing her degree, Colleen moves back. She and Mary decide to share an apartment.

But something is different between them now. They feel a tension in their relationship. Each of them realizes, independently, that she is attracted to the other woman. Their friendship develops into something deeper. Both of them find this frightening and disturbing. They do not know what to do with the feelings they have for one another. They struggle with this attraction for two years and finally they accept it for what it is. Then they decide to make a commitment to one another.

Some of the women in the group nod, some cry. One couple in the room has lived a similar story. Some of them were present when Colleen and Mary had their commitment ceremony at the local Metropolitan Community Church. Someone talks about how Colleen and Mary wanted to have a ritual because they were Catholic; they wanted to experience mystery, celebrate this life event, and bring their love to God, whom they always experienced as a part of their relationship.

Not only is the story of Mary and Colleen's relationship touching. On this sunny February afternoon it provides us with the space and a vessel for the storytelling that arose from it.

What we had shared at our first meeting becomes alive in an entirely new way in this second meeting. When we express our stories in writing, our stories are sharper and clearer. Our feelings are stronger. I hear interesting expressions and a poetic turn of speech or two. Creativity abounds. Ideas encircle us. When I hear the feedback we give to one another, I can feel a new charge in the room as women glow with affirmation, smile from being encouraged, and scribble notes to themselves about changes they can make. They leave looking inspired!

One Holy Family

Joan Lafferty

Joan and her partner of twenty-nine years are raising their sixteen-year-old daughter. Between working and keeping up with the life of a teenager, Joan continues to explore a variety of configurations for a spiritual community. Like any valuable relationship, Joan's spiritual partnership with the Roman Catholic Church has its "for better and for worse" periods; lifelong partnerships are bound to have their ups and downs. In the course of her life journey, Joan continues to strive for patience and compassion toward spiritual fulfillment.

About twenty years ago I answered a knock on my apartment door to find a woman dressed in a black dress with black shoes in the scorching heat of an August day. She smiled maternally at me and asked if I would like to learn more about God's love for me. If I didn't already have a church, she would like to share some scripture passages with me and talk about my life. Facing her on my own stoop, I uncharacteristically blurted out, "I am a homosexual Catholic. I just can't talk to you about this right now."

We stared at each other for several minutes and she finally said, "Well, I'll be praying for you." As she turned to leave, she added, "God loves you too."

I wanted to call her back and have her tell me again until I believed it. She was kind, more kind than I had been to myself and much kinder than I had allowed others to be. By this time, I had been in my relationship with Jane for three years, and I knew that it was not a phase, an inclination, or unnatural for me. But I also knew the church's teaching on homosexuality. Looking back on that somewhat random encounter, I realize that it has, in many ways, shaped my journey in the church and in my own skin.

During that time, Jane and I hid our relationship from everyone who was not part of our small gay community. We had withdrawn from our parish community, fearing that parishioners would shun us if they knew us too well. When I spoke so brashly to the woman on my front stoop, I had expected rejection and disgust. Instead, she was the first person outside of our small group of gay friends that I told, and it had gone pretty well. Maybe I could begin to let people know, even people in my own church.

Jane and I met in 1983 when we lived in a Catholic volunteer community. Jane was a social worker in a Catholic agency assisting the poor with food, clothing, heating, employment, etc. I was a teacher in a Catholic school. There were six of us in community that first year with similar jobs—all young and trying to live out our Catholic faith.

As years passed, Jane and I—individually and together—learned what it meant to be in a long-term relationship and to be included in a rich and loyal community of friends who would stand up for us through all adversity. We also discovered the pain that comes with first being invisible and then scorned by a church that did not want to know us and could not accept us. As we became more comfortable with our life together, our very presence at Mass became a source of controversy. As we changed from being totally closeted, which we came to recognize as the lie it was, we were a persistent challenge to the other parishioners. We neither sought nor enjoyed the role of agitator, and so we left.

We prayed and discerned and talked, but in the end, we left. And in the years that followed, we separated from the church that we loved and for which we worked. We railed against our beloved community, much like a disappointed teenager rails against the family she so desperately loves.

In time, we began to ask ourselves if this was how God loves us and how God's people show their love for us. We began to ask ourselves if our leaving the church was better. Did it enrich our prayer life? Had we built a stronger community? Were we better people? Also, was the church better off for our having left? Was the controversy we created outside of the church's capacity for community?

And so, we tentatively began our journey back to the family of the church that we missed, that bore our faith, and that we loved. As we did, we agreed to be honest from the start. We agreed to open our lives to our community. We agreed to accept the words that the woman had spoken to me on my front stoop: God loves us too.

When we decided to invite a child to become part of our family, we had been together thirteen years and had come out to our families, friends, coworkers, and, most importantly, our parish. This is a process that is monumental to gay people, a process that involves a journey into real self-discovery. It includes asking questions such as "Who am I in this world and in God's creation? Am I deserving of a place at the table? Can I be loved for who I am?"

Our coming-out process began with prayer; it transformed us from fear and self-loathing to loving acceptance, and it ended with further prayer. For many, the coming-out process can be crystallized in a few peak moments, some difficult, some beautiful, and all enduring. We had our peak moment in our parish.

Before we left for China to bring home our daughter, the parish gave us a blessing. As these parishioners, some of whom we barely knew, walked forward out of their pews to lay hands on us and sing us a blessing, Jane and I cried and released all of the ways that we had ever felt abandoned and rejected and scorned by the church that had once loved and nurtured and educated us. We knew that, once we brought our daughter home, this parish would give to her all the love and hope and challenge that we had felt as children in a Catholic parish.

We have not been disappointed. Jane and I continue to marvel at the grace by which our parish embraces our family in the sacramental life of the community. As we prepared for Mei's baptism, we prayed that she would feel the acceptance of a community that loved her unconditionally. When she received her First Holy Communion, we prayed that she would recognize Jesus incarnate in herself and others. When she prepares for confirmation, we will continue to pray that she embody the church's compassionate tradition of service to the poor. We will pray that she can rely on the church's teachings to guide but not rule her life and that she will be directed by an internal authority nurtured by the Holy Spirit.

Most people want to know if Mei's school friends know that she has two moms, how her classmates treat her, and if there has been any difficulty. We often tell other gay friends that, if you are not "out of the closet" before you have a child in your life, you will be shortly thereafter. From the time that she could talk, Mei has been introducing us as her two moms to anyone who was near: waitresses, grocery store checkout clerks, other amusement-park riders at Silver Dollar City, etc. She has never known anything about shame or secrets.

Mei had one incident at her Catholic school. As the second grade class was preparing for First Communion, another classmate told Mei that she could not be Catholic because her parents were gay. Mei responded that Jesus welcomes everyone to the table. She understands. Am I happy about her response? Yes. Would I rather that she did not have to give it? Yes, again. Still, Mei knows who she is, and, if you ever have the chance to meet her, you will know what a healthy, happy, and giving person she is.

As Catholics, Jane and I share a love for and knowledge of our church, its teachings, traditions, and history. We want to pass this on to our daughter. In the twenty-three years of our partnership, that love and knowledge has sustained us, both individually and as a couple. We want Mei to have this same type of sustenance. Sometimes the road has been difficult, as we have felt scorned and abandoned. Still, we have never doubted in that time that God knows and loves us, that our community knows and loves us, and that we know and love each other.

We continue to engage in loving opposition to the church teaching that the homosexual life, fully lived by two adults who have made a life-long commitment to each other, is intrinsically evil and disordered. We know this to be an unfortunate misinterpretation of our God's sacred scripture and the church's loving tradition. We look at Mei and witness the security that she experiences in her home and the love that she takes for granted in her relationships. We know that bringing her into our life was not the same as doing violence to her, as one recent church document claimed. We allow our community to remind us that the hurtful words, written by those who have never met us, do not represent their feelings or beliefs; our community tells us every day, in every way, that they know us and love us and value us. They say what the stranger on my stoop said to us: that they will pray for us and that God loves us too.

Finding God, Finding Myself

Cathy Luebbering

Cathy enjoys live music, is an idealist at heart, loves good food (of the vegetarian variety) and conversation, and is grateful for the journey.

In seeking to capture the essence of my spiritual journey as a woman who, in recent years, identifies as lesbian, I look back and see my path as strongly influenced by my father and childhood experiences. As a child, I felt I could never quite reach my father—either physically or emotionally. In my mind's eye, I see myself walking with him to the backfields, my sisters and I trying to match his pace by stepping into his footprints. We couldn't keep up, but that didn't keep us from trying!

I remember my father walking through the kitchen, headed outside, hunched over and silent, with a grave facial expression. This was common, for he was serious by nature, and very private. That somber demeanor has taken me years to understand. Now I see that it embodied a sense of guilt, shame, and unworthiness. I believe that my dad communicated nonverbally what he held deep within—that God was a punishing, judgmental, and distant presence whom he feared. I gradually absorbed this powerful message as I tried to connect in some meaningful way with my father and, later, in seeking a personal relationship with God.

Raised Roman Catholic, I learned and committed to memory the prayers taught in my catechism classes. I faithfully repeated these words at night, just as my mother had taught me and my siblings to do. Though I said the words, in my heart I felt no connection to God through this practice and, eventually, I stopped praying in this rote way because it lacked meaning for me.

I recall my confirmation as a time when I first realized a desire to know God more personally. I could not voice or articulate that budding desire. My family did not discuss or encourage the expression of feelings, and I had no words for what was stirring within. I knew that going to church, in itself, was not especially satisfying and, at times, felt more like a duty than an opportunity for connecting in a meaningful way with God. But there were positive experiences. I remember appreciating the warmth, affection, and concern that a particular priest displayed toward me and other children. And later, when I sang in the choir, singing became my prayer and remained so for many years.

I am third oldest in a family of nine children. My parents instilled in me that my duty was to put others first—that life was about sacrificing for others' sake. Years later I realized that by accepting that duty and by having to assume a parental role as a child, I was not able to explore life in my own unique way, to find my own rhythm for moving through the world. Having neither parent to confide in, I felt lost and confused during my childhood and adolescent years.

I began therapy as a young adult and, in time, I realized that my emotional health was closely entwined with my spiritual journey. Healing my emotional wounds has been the motivation for much self-reflection and spiritual healing as an adult. I participated in traditional therapy for many years; afterward, I found alternative healing approaches and developed an appreciation for journaling, meditation, massage, Reiki, Healing Touch, Native American sweats and vision quests, the wonder of nature, spiritual direction, and trusted friends.

I learned to surrender the burdens I had taken on as a child. I learned that life is about seeking out, and listening to, my own inner wisdom. I discovered God in light-hearted moments and experiences and found that what brought me great joy, wonder, and a sense of freedom was exactly where God wanted me to be!

I finally could hear the message of "Come, meet me in these joyful moments; I am here." Surprisingly, I heard this message in a most clear and powerful way when I chose to take swimming lessons a few years ago. I had previously been terrified of the water, but I decided to walk into this fear. I found an instructor whom I trusted and who worked with me at my pace while also challenging me to push myself farther than I thought I could go. Although it's been about seven years ago, I remember those early days and am moved by Cindy's ability to work with me and help me to discover great joy in that YWCA pool. When I finally could go into the deep end, I found I could be held by the water. And not only was I held by the water—I found I was being held by my Creator! Words cannot describe the wonder I found in these experiences. I was finally opening myself to explore the power, strength, and beauty of my own body, and I delighted in this new awareness. I grew to love swimming under the surface of the water, where I found God very much alive, calling me to return again and again. It was, and is, so empowering to move from fear into trust, and I knew that God had brought me to this place.

It was while I was learning about Native American spirituality and rituals that I developed a friendship with Nancy. Over the course of months, we spent time together, worked together, shared personal stories and meals with friends, and participated in a number of retreat experiences. She was already steeped in Native American spirituality, and she introduced me to the beauty of Native drumming; the cleansing, sacred prayer of Native American sweats; the practice of honoring the four directions by working with the medicine wheel; and other sacred rituals.

In time, I came to realize that this was a special relationship, something more than friendship, that Nancy was someone with whom I could share my story in a sacred way. Slowly, like pieces of a puzzle coming together, questions from prior dating experiences surfaced, and for the first time I understood why I had not been able to trust the men I dated or to commit myself to marry any of them. It was *Nancy* who was my first love, whom I was naturally and easily drawn to and with whom I shared much of myself so openly. What a sense of freedom and joy I felt—feelings I had not known in other intimate relationships. God was working within me to understand something new and exciting about myself, who I was created to be in this world. Although we are no longer together, Nancy and I shared much joy in worshipping and singing together at Mass, exploring nature, building friendships, sharing our spiritual journeys with one another, and growing individually and together.

Along with feelings of excitement and wonder, I have also experienced trepidation and fear with this new self-awareness. This brings me to another practice that has helped me to change and grow: centering prayer. I am naturally attracted to the silence and practice of going within, seeking oneness with my Creator through this form of prayer. I am learning to trust this sacred Presence as I am held in quiet solitude, held as I gradually, slowly surrender all that I cannot control. I can walk along this journey, embracing my sexuality, because I have experienced the love of my Creator, my God who loved me into being. I am grateful for the many friends who, by their example, teach me how to embrace the truth of my identity. I am humbled by their journeys.

As a person who has felt on the outside of life, I am gradually finding comfort in understanding that I am a spiritual seeker. It's in my blood, my bones, and my soul. I cannot imagine life any other way. I am open to experiencing and understanding God in many ways and, in so doing, I have set aside my father's image of the divine. God is no longer distant and far from me. God is the Beauty and Power of nature, a quiet voice within, showing feminine and masculine traits. God awaits me with tender, loving arms, accepting me fully, just as I am. God is alive in my daily experiences with others, and She speaks to me through my work, and through music, poetry, art, conversations with others, and many wonderful readings. I find that I can lean on a Divine Presence within who cares for me, but who challenges me to grow beyond my often limited view of myself and others.

Today I continue to seek opportunities for inner healing, knowing myself more deeply, and experiencing God in new and exciting ways. I recognize a need to keep working on setting healthy boundaries, opening up to really feel my feelings, and communicating my needs in a healthy manner. I believe that, as I continue this healing work, I will continue to open my heart more fully to God, myself, and all who are in my life. I do not have to prove myself to anyone, becoming distracted by what others might want from me. Today I understand my first responsibility is to myself, to honor my truth, live with integrity, heal past wounds, and experience the many joys of life. In reflecting back on the pain and confusion of my youth, I would never have dreamed I could be in a space of loving God by loving myself and experiencing such joy and delight in this knowledge.

A Metamorphosis of Faith

Catherine M. Kelley

Catherine has worked for more than thirty years as a social worker counseling adolescents, adults, and families; most recently walking with those at the end stages of life in hospice. She lives with her partner of eighteen years, their dog Lillie and cat Noah in the rural, college town of Northfield, Minnesota.

I am Catherine Margaret Patricia Kelley, born in 1953 into an Irish Catholic family on St. Patrick's Day. I attended Catholic schools from first grade through graduate school. At age twenty-three, I entered the religious order of the Sisters of St. Joseph and lived with them for eleven years. I received a bachelor's degree in social work from a Catholic women's college, and later a master's degree in social work from a Jesuit university. I have been ministering to children, adults, and families for the past thirty-three years in that profession.

Anyone reading the above paragraph would have some definite ideas about my beliefs, values, and spiritual journey thus far, and some of those presumptions would be fitting. Now, imagine that I am a lesbian woman in a committed relationship with another woman for the past seventeen and a half years. What changes in this life story?

Nothing *should* change; however, I have been treated and regarded much differently because of being a lesbian...not by family, not by friends, not by colleagues, not by neighbors, and not by God. But what about the church, in which I was baptized, confirmed, received First Communion, and made vows to as a woman religious? The Catholic Church no longer welcomes me "at the table" unless I'm a single, celibate lesbian woman. The church will only give me Communion as long as I stay closeted and deny who I really am. I did that for twenty-two years, and lived in a constant state of fear, shame, guilt, and suicidal ideation. Unfortunately, the church is no longer a source of spiritual nourishment for me, and I live each day feeling the sadness and grief of that loss.

Now the good news! My soul and my spirit know and experience faith, hope, love, strength, justice, peace, and communion with all that is good and sacred. This happens when I pray each day, go on retreats, walk in nature, sit by the water, listen to music, feel compassion toward others, love and respect others. It happens because of the many people in my life who love compassionately, live justly, and walk humbly with the HOLY each day. It happens because I am a better person being in the relationship with my life-partner than being a single, celibate lesbian woman.

My faith is unwavering, my prayers are constant, my commitment to social justice is strong; however, my worship in a community of faith leaves something to be desired. My partner and I have made a commitment to worship together in faith communities that are open, affirming, and welcoming of all persons who want to nourish their faith and grow in their spirituality. We have found the United Church of Christ to be one such denomination. My partner knows the importance of my heritage and has attended Catholic Mass with me on holidays and special events that the Sisters of St. Joseph have hosted. My sadness, anger, and feelings of abandonment about the Catholic Church's rejection of me are *always* beneath the surface when I am attending other faith communities and/or when attending Eucharistic liturgies in Catholic worship space.

My partner and I will continue to be seekers of communities of faith that truly live out the gospel message of unity and reconciliation. I take comfort in the following words from *The Celtic Spirit*, a daily meditation book that is part of my spiritual practice.

> *"Wherever we are in our spiritual search, we must each worship according to the needs of our heart and nature. To do other than this is to betray our soul. But it is not an easy path."*

> *"The fact that there is not only one (or even any) right way and the possibility that our spiritual questing may not have an ultimate solution or destination is hard to accept. We can only follow our heart's leading to our soul's home."*

My prayer is that each one of us may travel the path that will fulfill our soul's destiny.

A Spiritual Journey

Dorothy L. Calvani

Dorothy is often surprised by joy…be it in the mountains, by the ocean, on city streets, or in the eyes of those with whom she shares life. Striving to hear the "lub-dub" of each heartbeat as a "thank-you," she joins with so many others to act justly, to love tenderly, and to walk humbly with our inclusive, banquet-giving God.

"You fill us with life and goodness; You bless us and make us whole."

I have two really big dimples, so big, in fact, that as I age they seem to be meeting under my chin, giving me the appearance of a chinstrap penguin. I have a birthmark that covers twenty-five percent of my body and when I'm cold it turns deep purple. I once was honored with the "Nurse Practitioner of the Year" award for my contributions to our statewide professional organization. I'm real proud of that. I sing with the Threshold Choir, a group offering "bedside singing" to those who are sick, lonely, or dying. I make quilts for every newborn that comes along in our network of family and friends. I love to cook and to eat. I ride a bike to work and hike as much as possible. I prefer mittens to gloves. I feel extraordinarily blessed by our nurturing earth. I am a Catholic with Celtic tendencies and Italian passions. I am in the thirty-third year of a most loving relationship. I am a lesbian, a "happy, gay, and well-adjusted" lesbian. And this is a story of how my unique spirit has traveled with the gift of life offered so lovingly to me from my beginning.

Where to start? Many years ago, I wrote a piece about my "spiritual journey." It was at a time when I had finally emerged from a stressed, secretive place to a place where I began to understand the freedom and unconditional love offered to me and to all of us. This was my view in or about 1989:

I come from a small New England town. It was a place of both sweetness and pain. There was love, sure and solid; there was also mental illness and alcoholism. There are good memories and challenging ones. Into my reality came an insistent call. I was led away from that home by a miraculous tug to dedicate my life to God. I felt called to be with the poor, those who needed to know they were loved despite all earthly evidence to the contrary. Now I know it was I who needed that message most of all.

I entered the novitiate, a kind of school for young women wishing to be members of a religious community. It was a magical place full of silence and laughter, struggle and joy. It was a breath of fresh air for me and gave me a solid family where I could grow and develop. I loved the strong women's community, forged in sacred convictions. I loved the habit that made me a visible part of the group. In due time, I joyfully offered, and God accepted, my vows to belong to God alone. It was a moment of pure rapture.

I moved into several "mission" houses where the nitty-gritty work of the community took place. I nursed, advocated for, and loved people who welcomed me into their homes and hearts. They were poor, marginalized, and often without hope; sharing life with them was a privilege for which I am eternally grateful. They formed and blessed me in ways I will never completely understand. Once professionally trained, I became a fully prepared member of the community. I was twenty-four years old, and for the first time—despite my joy in our work—I had some doubts about living my commitment forever. I was becoming restless but could not look it in the eye and understand the roots of my growing discontent.

As life would have it, during this period, I received a profound message in prayer. It was a deeply felt understanding that no matter what would happen to me, even if earth passed away, God would be with me. At that moment, I had no idea how significant this embodied inspiration was, nor was I aware how much I would need this message in times to come.

Years passed and it was time to make final vows. I felt that in order to make this serious commitment honestly, I first had to know what it was to be an "independent" agent, an experience that I had never had. Secondly, I had developed a close friendship with a woman, with whom, unbeknownst to me, I had fallen in love. I requested a leave of absence from the community. Surprisingly enough, the details of our early relationship were not dramatic; I had no previous knowledge of my sexual orientation, nor did I perceive that I was leaving the community "for a woman."

Today I know that my life was, and always has been, women-centered. The fact that I slowly came to understand that I AM lesbian, that my spiritual energy dances to this beat, further demonstrates to me an essential truth: I was on a path that would gently and lovingly lead me to understand that the Divine Mystery has no favorites! I was trained to think that there was some kind of formula for eternal acceptance, i.e., Catholic, religious, straight, etc. It's simply not true. It took many radical incidents in my life to teach me the truth. That is, I learned that listening carefully to one's inner experience and living with integrity the call that the experience inspires is the only "formula" that may exist to put us where we need to be.

I then found my home with the woman who has blessed my life ever since with love, trust, and a profound sense of gift. Those early days were filled with pain, confusion, and guilt. Once the "lesbian light" began to dawn, darkness moved in! My father would kill me! How could I be one of those? I couldn't even speak the word. I was terrified. I made my leaving the community final. I searched for, found Dignity, and then finally, one night, I said it out loud while washing dishes with a gay man at a women's homeless shelter. "I'm a lesbian," I told him. I waited for the ceiling and sky to fall, and nothing happened except he gave me a hug and said, "That's wonderful!"

As I grew stronger about affirming my lesbianism, it all began to fall into place. How could God who had always guided me, folded me in mercy, and stayed with me even in the roughest of times, abandon me? What a cruel Divine joke it would be to create me lesbian then judge me negatively for being one. My experience of a loving God was not consistent with a God who would reject me. I remembered my revelation so long ago…"I am with you," even if my church, family, or my entire culture is not.

It was a long, slow road coming out to my family. It was in the eleventh year of our relationship that I had *the* conversation with my father on the phone. He hung up on me. That was the beginning of a long painful period during which he refused to speak to me, carrying his rage and personal hurt as far as threatening my partner's life. My mother's love was constant, but could not overshadow this paternal tempest. Interestingly enough, with this dramatic cut-off, something amazing happened—I was set free! I was no longer a prisoner of a shameful secret. For the first time in a long time, I felt whole.

It is often very hard to believe, deep down in our inner core, that we are loved—that we truly belong. But this I have come to know, not because of what I do or don't do, not measured by my ability or weakness, but because God is an eternal banquet-giver and invites *everyone* to the table equally. I belong; we all belong. Thank you and let us say Amen, so be it!

What has happened in the intervening years? How has this journey continued? For one thing, the One beyond all names has grown bigger and bigger and more inclusive and earthier and juicier and sweeter, seemingly, in some ways, as our Roman Catholic Church has gotten narrower, more punitive, and less tolerant.

Going back a bit, I must admit there was a time when I was very angry with Jesus—Jesus, the *man* who, with the deeply judging Father, I had clearly associated with the disgust in my own father's heart and the official teaching of the Catholic Church about my "intrinsic disorder." Despite the feeling of abandonment and pain, this was an extremely important phase of my learning, of my being formed in new and ancient truths; it still is vital. By losing the authoritarian Jesus, the patriarchal Jesus, I had lots of latitude to find Jesus, the human expression of Incarnation. He is the One (in my spiritual tradition) who came willingly as the continuation of the Word spoken in the primordial "big bang" that began the ever-expanding divine dimensions of creation, of life. As far as I can see, the historical life of Jesus, contrary to more fundamentalist understandings, was one that bore witness to the dismantling of so called "purity laws"; who said that He had come to show that the "reign" of God, the expression of God is in each of us, particularly when we are humble and grateful; and who showed that loving deeply, unconditionally, may bring suffering and death, and through death, a new life.

Jesus, the Christ, is a different person/reality for me now compared to the person/reality He was in my youth. This was and is a long and complicated metamorphosis, but perhaps a short "parable" would be a good example of this perspective change. During the Easter season, we are reminded of the story of the "miraculous catch" of John 21:1-14. There are the depressed and frightened friends of Jesus fishing. They are not having much luck. A "stranger" on the shore suggests they cast their nets in a different direction, and they are abundantly rewarded. John recognizes "the Lord," and Peter leaps from the boat, swimming in exaltation toward his cherished friend. The scene switches to a charcoal fire crackling with a fish cooking on it and bread waiting. There is chef Jesus on the shore, having prepared this tender welcome and sure evidence of being alive.

Of course there are many ways to interpret this beautiful story. What strikes me at first is how often we are looking in the wrong places for understanding and how we need some major shake-up in our old and familiar ways in order to move us in a different direction. In my own life the major shake-up involved my gradual discovery of myself as a lesbian. Some would regard this realization as the worst possible news but, on the contrary, it has been the Divine's way of leading me to unconditional love.

Second, an image of the divine emerges from that parable—a God who is delighted to sensitively and abundantly nurture us just like a mom or a grandma or some wonderful woman in our lives. Jesus, a cook, a grandma…YES! More than that, the partner in an ever-widening, loving, and unconditional relationship not based on judgment but on burning desire and forgiveness.

"You fill us with life and goodness."

What has nourished these growing clarities?

There are so many influences that happen to me everyday—those "hundred million miracles" for which I am eternally grateful. I believe I stand on the shoulders of stars, ancestors, relatives, friends, and all social-justice workers who give me strength and consolation. We are what we have been given. What we make of "our one precious life" is our unique blessing, responsibility, and legacy, held in the grace and wisdom of compassion's hands. Clarissa Pinkola Estes suggests that whoever we help in their struggle or pain bears our fingerprints on their souls forever.

Among the influences that continually help my spirit on this journey are, strangely enough, some of the "open-fire" modes of the institutional churches. Somehow, experiencing the pronouncements on and judgments about my lesbian nature has made me dwell on these matters fiercely, and thus I have come to realize how profoundly they do not fit with my relationship to the Divine.

"You bless us and make us whole."

The New Cosmology/creation spirituality has provided me with mountains of joyful nourishment. How can I explain how the three guiding principles of Gaia have thrilled my soul? Having come to see how "interiority, diversity, and communion" explain the essence of all life, I cannot help but rejoice for myself and my earth family. Think about it…what would the world be like if we sincerely understood and respected the facts that *every* part of Creation is distinctly unique and essential, beautifully differentiated from each other, and intrinsically connected? This has opened my heart to the universe, to the earth, and to all nature in the most wondrous of ways. Our continued existence depends on our collective conviction that we go into the future together reverencing all life, animate and inanimate, or not at all. For me, this is a call to live my life humbly proud and grateful, knowing that my little tiny speck of a life matters, that all life's expression matters. It is in how I stay in right relationship to all life that matters.

"You fill us with life and goodness, You bless us and make us whole."

Thank God for the many theologians, scholars, and women who put their lives on the line studying, writing about, and living the feminine aspects of God and elucidating the nonsexist core of the Divine! This feminist perspective is so vital in our time of rampant testosterone, hierarchical thinking, and renewal of draconian measures to keep women in traditional roles and out of places of decision. Women's nature to "gather and tend" lifts up everyone, the entire human family, male and female alike. How happy am I to live at a time when there is historical, mystical, and emotional "evidence" that to be a woman is important, creating a particular place in the household of the One.

"You bless us and make us whole."

Gratefully, our time in history has gifted us with the invitation to enjoy ecumenism. The Divine is not limited by my Christian faith. On the contrary, the many spiritual threads in our world all lead to the One. Many of these traditions and "ways of looking" have deeply enriched my own perspective. In particular, I "bow in gratitude and compassion" to my Native American relatives, my Buddhist relatives, my Celtic relatives, and the four-legged ones (especially my cat Ringo Starr)—among others—who have added so much to my process.

"You fill us with life and goodness."

For me, spiritual mentoring, spiritual direction, involvement in reflection groups, and opportunities to make ritual with others are such important means to grow, bloom, and thrive. For example, I have the most amazing spiritual director. Her extraordinary abilities of empathic listening and sacred insights midwife and help me access the stream of God's grace that heals, renews, and sets my soul on fire. Of course this process is not easy. Growing in self-knowledge may be one of the most difficult things any of us ever attempts. But I know no better way of finding the call to compassion for others than to learn the truth about one's own "ego-antics" along with one's strengths and weaknesses, gifts and black holes. Wonder of wonders? God is in them all, forming and transforming! The Presence often shines brightest in the darkness. True, it can be a roller-coaster ride, yet, without it, I would be missing one of the most profound rides of my life!

"You fill us with life and goodness, You bless us and make us whole."

The living God calls me to find ever more jubilant ways to celebrate! To this day, there remain storms—everywhere—that whip at the hearts, minds, and bodies of LGBT people. God knows, we are not the only ones. There are legions of people who do not fit the criteria of someone else's "acceptable"—the poor, the immigrant, the old, the stranger, those who are challenged in other ways. For too many of us, these times can be devastating, dangerous, and/or deadly. Nonetheless, we must always and in everything, try to find ways to walk together in order for the kingdom, the household of God, to vibrate with the song of one family.

For me, this celebrating takes some specific forms. Foremost, participating in the Eucharist and seeking to live a Eucharistic life is an essential. How are we to be given the strength, like the Bread broken, to break open ourselves and, like the Wine shared, to pour out our lives, if we are not nurtured at this table of endless belonging? In recent times, our church has suggested that "practicing" LGBT persons voluntarily refrain from receiving Communion. This suggestion, in my opinion, is not only misguided, it is beyond cruel, and it is impossible. Can this come from the heart of God?

Another type of celebration is the forming and carrying on of the Bee Winkler Weinstein Fund. This is a fund that assists lesbian, bisexual, and transgendered women, 18-25 years of age, who have been disowned emotionally and/or financially by their families. Its origin is in the experience of paternal rejection. The money that began the fund was a fraction of what should have been my partner's inheritance after her father's death. Her father had made it clear that our relationship precluded dividing his estate fairly. This money felt like a slap rather than a parental embrace. After pondering for some time, we agreed that we would begin a fund to help other young, disenfranchised women, in order to somehow redeem this dreadful situation. We ultimately found that building and caring for this fund gives us a deep sense of solidarity and sharing. It gives me a sense of gratitude and compassion for the one who, in life, could not enjoy us but, in death, could provide us with the means to participate in our community in a way we could never have imagined.

The joyful celebration continues in a current project that honors LGBT elders. Three of us have developed a workshop series entitled: LGBT ElderSpirit: Savoring our Lives©. This project recognizes the matured inherent resilience and spirit in our elders. LGBT persons over the age of 60 have lived through some of the most amazing times in LGBT history. With a core storytelling format, the participants are invited to take a look back over their lives to help them know more clearly their personal strengths, the strengths that have made surviving and thriving possible in spite of adversity. What a privilege to, in some small fashion, support honoring the strength, power, and wisdom of our elders. What mutual treats for all!

I truly believe that the celebration will grow stronger and wider and deeper. How could it not? The Creator of this beautiful universe infinitely delights in all creation. What better way for the Divine to speak delight than to help us continually find the means to say thank you?

"This I believe: I shall see the goodness of God in the land of the living."

In this gift of Life, I continually circle back to the beginnings, the promise that no matter what, God is and will be with me, with us all. Jesus told Nicodemus that the Spirit is like the wind—one has no idea where it comes from or where it is going, but one feels it nonetheless. Surely, my life is a work-in-progress carried by the Spirit's breeze. Surely, the power and intimacy of a thirty-three-year loving relationship continues to reveal the sweetness and mercy of God to me. Surely, tears and joys will continue to be a gifted part of my life, your life. For certain, I have begun to experience the blessing of a sort of freedom that feels like pure grace. Always, a sense of gratitude continues to spread throughout each day. No doubt we belong—our whole Earth family—to a God beyond all names or imagination. How I hope that you, the reader, profoundly experience this beautiful mystery. I bow in a deep sense of reverence to you and pray:

> *May you be at peace,*
> *May your heart remain open,*
> *May you know the beauty of our own true nature,*
> *May you be healed,*
> *May you be a source of healing for all beings. Amen.*

> — From the Buddhist meditation practice "Mehta"

Reflections...

In the Beginning was the Voice

When I was a child we had a family Bible. It had a brown leather cover with engraved gold surrounding the words, Holy Bible. There were pictures throughout depicting the more dramatic stories of the Bible. The edges were trimmed in gold. In the Gospels, the words spoken by Jesus were written in red. It had a place in the front where we could keep family records of births, marriages, and deaths. I loved sitting on my dad's lap and looking at the Bible. He would make comments on the pictures and the passages of scripture that they represented.

We let my aunt borrow our Bible at one point in my childhood, and she kept it at her apartment for years. When I was about fifteen, I decided I wanted to read the Bible each night before I went to bed. I asked my dad to request its return from my aunt, his sister. When I got the Bible, I kept it in my room, and that began my lifelong love affair with reading scripture.

Like all love affairs, this one has had its ups and downs. For some years I decided I could no longer read the Bible during prayer. I kept coming upon passages that I became angry with after reading them. I was in my thirties by this time and reading feminist theology and just becoming aware of the injustice of patriarchy and the many ways in which it touched my life. So I gave up on the Bible for a while. I could not buy into an angry Jesus who preached woe to his enemies, who tricked his disciples with riddles, and who insulted them by telling them they had little faith.

Then I got involved with lesbian, gay, bisexual and transgender ministry. I studied scripture and prayed with a community of gay men and lesbian women, and I prepared homily hints for our pastor at the parish. What I noticed about our praying with scripture was that as members of our community shared about their lives, it didn't matter what the scripture was, they talked about being accepted or, more often than not, not being accepted by the church that was and is family to them. We prayed over the lectionary readings every time we met. It didn't matter what the message of the reading was, we could find Jesus's message of inclusive love and his compassion for those on the margins in every passage.

As the weeks began to add up to several months, I started to see scripture through the eyes of those on the margins, and I have not been the same since. I see Jesus reaching out to those in need. I see the paradox of the world being turned upside down in favor of those at the bottom of society. I find myself identifying with those to whom Jesus ministers. Scripture has become a part of my everyday prayer experience once again. I find a deep, moving, and personal message when I read scripture. When I prepare prayers for our community or share a reading with my small church community, I find myself talking about God's love in a way that is similar to how Joan writes about it. God's love is unconditional, generous, and faithful.

When we started our gathering of women to cultivate and harvest stories for this book, scripture became a part of our time together. We gathered each time to share stories—some about God revealing God's self in the Bible. Some about God revealing God's self in our lives, as in Cathy's story, which speaks to us of God revealing new things to her in the simple acts of everyday life.

Opening up the Word and raising up of our voices became a sacred act at our gatherings and as we wrote. The Word and our voices blended together in one prayer, witness, and blessing. Familiar texts came alive in new and special ways, similar to Dorothy's description of the miraculous catch. Another example is the story of the man born blind, seen here through the lens of the lesbian and bisexual experience:

Jesus was asked if the man born blind was blind because of his sin or his parents'. The assumption was that if someone was disabled, it was a punishment for sin, so whose sin was responsible for this man's blindness? Jesus said neither: "He was born blind so that God's works might be revealed in him."

Often in our community people behave as if being lesbian or bisexual is the fault of that individual. Some even look to prenatal conditions or dysfunctional parenting practices for an explanation. Actually the explanation that Jesus gives applies here, too. This is a blessing from God. This condition reflects God's glory. It does not point to something wrong in our lives.

Another perspective on this story comes from the parents' response. The parents seem ambivalent—do they really want to own that this is their child and embrace him fully? This is something that all too many members of our community face with their parents. They can get strength from Jesus here. Parents who have suffered criticism for having a lesbian or bisexual daughter can, likewise, find strength in this story. They can enter into the story and picture themselves meeting Jesus. They too, can experience coming to believe in his healing power.

Other passages from scripture that reflect a theme of rejection overcome by the unconditional love of God include:

The stone that was rejected becoming the cornerstone; our community, rejected, being held in high esteem by God, and becoming finally recognized as the keystone of the community.

The Good Shepherd looking for the lost sheep because one hundred is a perfect number, and if one is missing, the community has only ninety-nine members and is no longer complete. To be a full faith community, we need everyone and we have to go find the other member because we are all lost without her.

We are all familiar with the passage about Jesus calling to Lazarus to leave the tomb. A common translation for this passage is: "Lazarus, come out." Coming out has a particular and special meaning in our community. And while I know that is not literally what Jesus meant, the verse has such a familiar ring and speaks of gay pride and being set free, that this is what I and many members of our community hear. Jesus also asks the community to approach Lazarus and unbind him. We need each other to be unbound. We need the support of our community to feel free. We need to unbind others so we, too, can be unbound. This is reflected in what Catherine says in her story about others teaching her to love.

Paul's letter to the Galatians has a verse about how we are no longer Gentile or Jew, slave or free, woman or man, but all one in Christ. This could also be applied to orientation as well as gender, we are no longer gay or straight, but we are one.

The Acts of the Apostles telling us about a major decision of the early church: should those who are uncircumcised be allowed to be Christian? This was a huge departure from early church tradition. Can understanding, acceptance, and outreach from the dominant community be extended to those who, because of sexual orientation, form a minority?

A particularly favorite passage of mine is from John's Gospel. I translate it to be more inclusive of orientation and gender, changing the Greek *logos*, meaning "word"—a static, masculine, legal concept that comes from the head—to "voice"—a dynamic, feminine aspect of speech and empowerment that is more fully embodied in head, heart, spirit, and flesh. Anne Perkins, who taught ancient Greek at Webster University for a number of years, has translated this passage from its original Greek for us, changing some nouns and pronouns to reflect the feminine gender of "voice."

In the beginning was the Voice,

And the Voice was face-to-face with God,

And the Voice was God.

At the very beginning she was alongside of God.

Through her all things were coming into being,

And apart from her nothing was coming into being:

She was the one who caused everything.

In her was life,

And the life was the light of humanity.

The light was shining in the darkness,

And the darkness did not overcome it...

The light was truth,

The light that shines on all

As it comes into the world.

She was in the world

And the world was made by her,

Yet the world did not recognize her.

To her own she came,

Yet her own people did not accept her.

But to those who did receive her

She gave the power to become

Children of God...

The Voice became flesh

And lived among us,

And we have seen her glory,

The glory of a newborn child

Coming from her mother,

Filled with grace and truth.

And from the fullness

We have all received

Grace upon grace.

HEALING

*There is no greater agony than
bearing an untold story
inside you.*

— *Maya Angelou*

Recollections...

Coffee House

We take some time off from our meetings in order for the women to spend more time writing. When we get together again, we are not able to meet at Jane and Joan's house, so we gather at a coffee house near where they live. Eight of us put three small tables together. The coffee shop is empty except for a young woman who comes in after we are settled. She sits just two tables over from us.

We talk for a while about writing, how hard it is. How it is easier to just talk about our lives. I offer to meet with members of our group one-on-one to interview them and transcribe what they have to say. No one takes me up on that.

We start to listen to the stories. Charlotte is reading to us about how no one at her school knows she is lesbian. She says she leads a double life. She does not talk about what she does over the weekend at work. As she is reading this, each of us glances cautiously toward the woman at the table, who is reading, but within hearing distance of us. Charlotte's voice becomes softer; she seems more tentative as she reads. I keep looking at the stranger who can hear us talk about the intimate details of our lives.

We listen to four stories. Everyone shares openly, even if cautiously. We hear Sylvia talk about meeting her partner and loving her deeply, how she met her on Holy Saturday and how that touches upon the sacred for her. We talk some about the pain of being judged by the leaders of our church. We share stories of being on guard and holding back even as we are on guard at the coffee house, yet none of us holds back. We tell our stories anyway.

Entangled with Love: Saying Good-bye is Never Easy

Kasey DeWitt

Kasey lives in Madison, Wisconsin, where she divides her time between working with college students, keeping up with a lively lab/dachshund mix named Lucy, marveling at a witty ten-year-old who constantly reminds her how to find spirituality in play, and a gracious partner who continues to amaze her with her tenacity. She continues the journey of saying goodbye to her mother and hello to life.

When I was ten years old, Ann Eckert invited me to her house for a sleepover on her birthday. When it was time for bed I felt intensely frightened, as often happened when I was away from my mom for too long. I jumped out of Ann's bed and went downstairs to ask Mrs. Eckert to take me home. Mrs. Eckert sat me down and told me how much I would be disappointing Ann if I left, and on her birthday, no less. I remember the guilt I felt for asking, the panic that increased throughout the night, as I lay awake worrying, and the relief I felt when I finally saw my mom the next morning.

Twenty years later I was again talking to Mrs. Eckert. "Kasey, it's time to come and see your mom."

"I can't see her like this. It's too hard," I replied.

"She's counting on you, and the doctors say she may not make it through the night."

As I hung up the phone, the same guilt and panic from when I was ten years old came flooding back. Except this time I couldn't run home to feel the relief of my mom's arms and words. She was counting on me, and I felt paralyzed.

My mom had been sick a lot when I was a child. Many of the illnesses were emotional, including one inpatient stay in the psych unit at our local hospital after my youngest brother was born. I worried about her dying constantly. I worried about me without her. At four years of age, all I knew was that my mom was taken away, and I was left with no mom. I remember going to bed each night of my childhood, listening to my parents arguing, and praying: "Please don't let her die." After that plea, I would talk to God about all sorts of other fears and concerns about my mom and dad. My mom taught me that God would be there, even when nobody else was. I told God that when my mom died, I wanted to go with her. I was so sure of it. During the day, I would try my best to listen to her problems and not to disappoint her by getting into trouble at school. We would often listen to music together, talk about our days, our emotions. I would tell her about things that happened at school, and she would tell me all about her childhood and about the time she was happiest—working in the music store in high school. Even though there were four other children, I felt like her special child, hearing her thoughts and feelings.

When I came out as a lesbian at the age of twenty-three, my mother was ready to listen and assure me of her love. She shared her concerns for my physical safety and for my place in the Catholic Church. Throughout the next few years we had many talks about how I (or if I) fit into the church. My life had been very much intertwined with the Catholic Church, and she saw me struggling with the doctrine. Mostly, being my mother, she saw the pain I went through trying to fit into a "home" that did not want to accept me or my love. Through it all, we challenged each other and listened to each other. After many years, my mother reached a point where she was able to say she only wanted my happiness. That was enough for me.

My mom had been smoking cigarettes since she was fifteen years old. She used to tell me that, from the first inhalation, something happened, and her nerves were calmed. Smoking calmed her like nothing else. In 1985, at the age of forty-nine, she was diagnosed with emphysema, the same disease that had killed her father ten years earlier. The doctors told her that, if she stopped smoking, they would put her on a list for lung replacement. I think she tried a few times, but she always told me there is nothing she loved more than the feeling of the smoke going down her throat. She could not do it. She tried carrot sticks, the patch, even hypnosis. Nothing worked because not having the cigarettes was worse than not being able to breathe. Addiction very slowly took hold of another body and soul.

She had already been in the hospital four days when Mrs. Eckert called—and I had not yet gone to see her. I thought about her every second of that time. This was her first major exacerbation since she was diagnosed. Because eight years had passed since the diagnosis and there had been no hospitalizations, I had convinced myself that this disease was manageable, and it would simply be a nuisance throughout her long life. When a disease progresses so slowly, it tricks you into thinking nothing is wrong. Now, here I was, suddenly faced with the thing I feared most in life—my mother's death. I was thirty years old, way too young to lose my mother, I thought. After I hung up the phone with Mrs. Eckert, defeated and terrified, I sat down on the floor and pleaded with God again, "Please don't let her die." The panic was fierce, and the shame of feeling paralyzed was even worse. I made a promise: "If you let her live, I promise I will work on letting her go." A few days later, they were able to wean her from the ventilator, and a few days after that, she went home.

Once my mom was home, I went to see her. I knew that she was disappointed in me for not visiting her in the hospital. I explained my fears about it, and she said she understood, but I knew her: she was deeply hurt. And I was ashamed. I found a therapist and began the work that was to bring both my mom and me to a place of peace. All the while I was fully aware that another exacerbation could kill her at any time. And there were more exacerbations, although not as severe as the first one. Throughout the next ten years, my mom was in and out of the hospital. With each stay I learned to visit her for a little bit longer. Each time after the doctors patched her up, the first thing she did was to reach for her cigarettes. During these years my focus was on trying to heal my fear of letting her go and to help her die a dignified death. Those were my noble goals, but what I found also happening was the desperate wish to somehow get her to stop smoking. I still do not know exactly why this was so important, because the disease had already progressed to a point where there was no turning back. I believed that, if she quit smoking before she died, it would somehow give her more dignity or strength. In actuality, it simply put a constant strain on our relationship.

On a late evening in February 2006, I got a call from my brother that the nursing home was sending my mom to the emergency room. The stent they inserted to dialyze her kidneys had become infected, and she was not doing well. This time I knew I had to go. I had promised God. When my partner and I got there, I looked into my mother's blue eyes. I still clearly see them looking back at me. I knew this was the beginning of the end. I do not know how, but I just knew. I panicked for about thirty minutes, called my siblings, and then went back in to sit with her. She was very spacey—both from the infection and from the toxins that had built up because her kidneys had not been flushed out. A few days later, when they tried to perform a dialysis, she had a reaction to the heparin. She began to bleed from every part of her body. The doctors did what they could and told us there was nothing more they could do. My sister stayed with her during that night. When I called to check in at 3:00 a.m., my sister said my mom just all of a sudden woke up hungry. She had made it through yet again. My partner went back to work, and I returned to stand vigil with my mother.

Now that she was awake, it was becoming evident that we needed to make a decision. The doctors could no longer use heparin, but because her kidneys were not working, her blood still needed to be purified. They tried to do it without the heparin, but my mom became extremely agitated and anxious. Without the heparin her blood clotted, making dialysis impossible. The night before they were going to try dialysis again, I asked my obviously anxious mom what it would be like if she did not have to ever have dialysis again. Her entire body relaxed, a huge smile came over her face, and she said, "It would be like heaven." I asked her if she knew what it meant to stop the dialysis, and she said she knew she would die without it, but she did not want to go through with it anymore. When we spoke to her doctors, her primary physician was upset and wanted to try more (even snake venom!) before they quit. We told the doctor it was time to stop. My siblings and I were relieved not to have to watch her suffer any longer.

The next day I brought my mom back to her nursing home to die. Before we got there, she had me pull into the Burger King parking lot so she could smoke a cigarette and drink a Coke Icee, her two favorite things. Throughout the next month, many friends and relatives came to visit and to say their good-byes. I took time off of work and was there with her almost every day. As the days went on, she became more confused and wanted me to be with her more. There were mornings I would come, and she would be angry, crying "Where were you?" I would hold her for a while and just let her cry. Then, composed again, she would ask me to take her out for a cigarette.

Four weeks later, April 11, 2006, she died very peacefully surrounded by most of her family. One of the first people I called was Mrs. Eckert.

So, it happened; she died. I was left alone to live. This did not set well with me at all. I was not that four-year-old who pleaded to God. I was forty and had been granted many more years with her than anyone thought possible. I should have been grateful. Instead, I felt like dying. My mind told me that my role on earth was to care for my mother, and now that role was gone, so I should be gone as well. This did quite a number on my six-year relationship with my partner, as I was really only able to concentrate on getting up each day and walking through my day. Obviously, I needed help with my grief. I sought out a therapist who got me in touch with a hospice group. In the group I was able to be honest about my sadness. I listened to others' sadness and triumphs in the darkest days of their lives. It empowered me to feel.

Since my mother's death the mysterious journey of grief that so many of us wander through has grabbed hold of me. The pain has been humbling and intense, bringing me to my knees more than once. I miss her deeply. Once in a while I feel her presence, or I hear her in my mind telling me she loves me. A couple of days after the funeral I was sitting at the pond by our condo crying. I looked up and there was a mother duck and her ducklings just watching me. Looking around, making sure no one was about to witness my silly behavior, I spoke to the mother duck. I shared my pain and fear. She just watched me, and I felt an odd sense of comfort. Sometimes now, when I am walking behind someone who is smoking, I close my eyes and take in a deep breath. I still keep a pack of her cigarettes in my glove compartment. Eventually I will throw them away, just not yet.

I used to think courage came from accomplishing great feats, and I'm sure it does. But the courage I found after my mom died came from just getting up and learning to live each day without her. There were many days I picked up the phone to call her only to realize she was no longer there. I began searching out "mother" stories. I encouraged my friends to tell me anything they could about their mothers. As the months went on, I started to understand that the fear I had of losing my mother had kept much of who I am trapped inside. I honestly thought my role in life was to make sure she was all right. Now she was gone, and I was left to live out my life by myself. I started to discover that I needed to find my own voice and become more honest with my emotions. My partner, unfortunately, did not want to take this part of the journey with me and decided to end our relationship. This was my first real test of standing on my own, without my mother to help pick me up.

My Christian faith told me that although death is sad, my mother would live forever in my heart and that the love would remain. This was no consolation to me, as I needed my mom's physical presence. I entered into a deep "darkness of the soul," and I found myself angry at God's cruel joke of making us to love each other, only to snatch us away from those we love.

There have been many days and nights where I have been tempted to die and join my mother. But for reasons I still don't fully understand, I've made the choice each day to live. And with each day, I find myself becoming stronger and more willing to feel life's twists and turns. I am finding my voice, learning how to dream, and standing taller. Although I have no proof, I am pretty sure my mom is helping me. I hope she is proud of me.

Spiritually, in the last three years since my mother's death, I have been challenged in more ways than I knew existed. I am still finding courage to actively search out who God wants me to be, and I'm coming to understand that I cannot/should not be in the business of trying to save people from their vices. God knows, I have my own to work with!

I have been a lifelong member of the Roman Catholic faith, earning my bachelor's and master's degrees in religious studies from a Sisninawa Dominican College. I have worked at a Catholic college the last nineteen years and have recently become a Dominican Associate. Yet, recently, in the wake of a new relationship, which includes a wonder-filled seven-year-old boy, I have decided to uproot and no longer call myself

Catholic. This decision has not come about lightly. I will always consider the Catholic Church my home. As a lesbian, though, and as a potential co-mother to a son, the Catholic Church does not want ME to fully participate in my home. I want Caleb to be proud of his family and to know God is also proud of us. I can cry about leaving, I can get angry, but in the end, I need to care for my spirit and step up to who God intends me to be. There is much work I need to do.

My Journey

Charlotte Webbe

Charlotte teaches elementary school children and spends her time with her partner enjoying a life together. She has joined the Episcopal Church and is very involved with the church. Once again, God answered her prayers with a welcoming, positive spiritual church.

I was a senior in high school when I realized for the first time that there were people who actually disagreed with what the Catholic Church taught. During a catechism class discussion on premarital sex, I was shocked as I watched a classmate arguing with our priest. It had never occurred to me that I could have my own beliefs and values that did not necessarily go along with the Catholic Church's teachings. Following the rules was simply part of the "deal." And, oh, the guilt if you didn't follow the rules!

Looking back, I can see how easy it was for me to simply accept things for the way they were. When I started questioning my sexuality, no wonder I felt so alone, so betrayed, so faithless, so angry, so guilty. People in my small town frowned on those who were "different." Why did I have to be different? What was I doing wrong? If I tried just a little harder, I could be just like everyone else. It would not be easy, but who said life was easy? But as hard as I tried to ignore it, being gay was not just going to go away. So I needed someone to blame. God. It was all God's fault. And fault it was. It was a burden, a blemish, an imperfection. In turn, that is what I believed I was. I was told that God didn't make mistakes, yet here I was.

During my early twenties, while working at a Christian-based summer camp, I came out to a friend, another camp counselor. We were both Catholic, often attending church together in a nearby small town. I admired her spirituality and trusted her opinions and values. She seemed to know the answers to many things. The whole camp seemed to center around her, or so it seemed to me. Looking back, I suppose I came out to her because I wanted her approval. I was mostly concerned about God and what this all meant for my spirituality. I felt like I had to choose between God and my sexuality. Although my friend said she could not tell me what God wanted, she told me to think of God like a grandparent. Many grandparents do not judge—they just love. They do not discipline harshly, and they are always happy to see you. What a concept! I had been told my whole life to fear God, and now I was being told to not be afraid of God. Could I imagine my grandparents *not* loving me? No. Well, God does not stop loving you no matter what. I have thought back to that conversation many times, and I believe it was a part of saving my spiritual life. However, at that point, I still was not convinced of God's unconditional love for me.

While living and teaching in a small town, I read online about PFLAG (Parents, Families & Friends of Lesbians and Gays). I was desperate. I was told that the next PFLAG meeting was in a few weeks. I felt nervous, but excited, as I waited for the weeks to pass. Before attending the first meeting, the parent I spoke with on the phone put me in contact with another lesbian who invited me to PRIDE that next weekend. It was a Saturday, and at that time PrideFest in my area was just getting underway. There were not very many people and only a handful of booths that day—Sunday was the big day. A small crowd was fine. Wearing a hat and sunglasses, I did not want to take the chance of either being on TV or running into someone I knew. People often seem to wonder why we need PRIDE weekends. What purpose do they serve? For me, it was truly the first time in my life where I did not feel like an outcast. I was not alone! I went back to the small town where I lived with a newfound feeling of worth.

Then I went to my first PFLAG meeting, and I met parents who actually celebrated their children being gay. I met parents who reminded me of my own parents. I was not out to my own parents, so those involved in PFLAG allowed me to hope that perhaps God had not abandoned me and maybe someday I could come out to my parents. I wanted to believe in their unconditional love, but I did not.

Through some parents I met in PFLAG, I found an inclusive Catholic Church. Like many Catholics, I did not want to break away from the church. It was all I knew, which, I realized over time, was part of the problem. When I went to my first Mass at this new parish, I was welcomed unconditionally. I only came out to a few people in the church, but I watched from afar the many people who were welcomed, no matter their life circumstances—divorcees, gays and lesbians, parents of adopted children, children and adults with special needs, single parents—you name it. The people in the church taught me that God has no boundaries. God offers everyone a seat at his table—all are invited to the feast. I cautiously stepped closer to God.

After attending PFLAG meetings and being part of a welcoming congregation for about a year, I was developing more hope and faith in God. Days before coming out to my parents, I decided to go and talk with their priest. Although I was not a big fan of his, my hope was that if I told him and my parents felt they needed some sort of spiritual guidance, he would know my "side." I had spoken with a gay man who had also spoken to this priest before coming out to his own parents. He encouraged me to see this priest because his experience with coming out to him was positive. Nervously I went to visit Father Steve. After telling him I was gay and about my concerns for my parents, his response was, "Well, I have friends too, but I don't go out and have sex with them." Needless to say, that meeting did not go as planned.

Later I had to wonder if, because they were two men talking, perhaps Steve was more understanding and compassionate with my gay male acquaintance. Frankly, I couldn't help but wonder if Steve is yet another closeted case leaving his parishioners to deal with his built-up anger for never having been brave enough to come out.

This is another reason why I am thankful that my spirituality had begun to flourish at that time. If I had not had the support of my church, PFLAG, and the memory of my camp friend's advice about God's unconditional love, I am afraid to think where the conversation with this priest may have put me. I was still cautiously stepping towards God, but I did not feel the abandonment I had felt for so long.

When my sisters and brother each moved in with their future spouses—before they were married—my mother went to pieces and thought for sure three of her four children would get struck down by a bolt of lightening. But when I came out to my parents, suddenly their other three children cohabiting before marriage didn't seem so bad.

"Of course we still love you!" my parents said when I came out to them. "Did you really think we were going to kick you out of the family? Disown you?" Well, frankly, yes, that's why I chose to tell them minutes before going back to my own apartment, an hour's drive away. Then, my die-hard Catholic dad said, "Well, I'm a little relieved. For a minute there I thought you were going to tell us you were going to join a convent to become a nun." Hmmm…it seemed that my being gay was the lesser of the two "evils." Would it have really been traumatic for his daughter to become a nun? Then my dad proclaimed that he blamed this whole gay thing on the women's movement in the 60s! WHAT??!?!?!

I am an elementary school teacher. At work, I believe I am a respected part of a powerfully dedicated staff of people who have devoted their lives to working with children. To my colleagues, I am an introverted, caring, positive, easygoing reading teacher. I do not share much about my life outside of my work. I keep conversations light, simple, and uncontroversial. I avoid gossip about other staff members, and I keep my nose clean. I have never been one to step out of line much. I am very careful about not causing waves, bringing little attention to myself. I do my job, and I do it well.

But I live a double life. Some may say I live a lie. Am I ashamed of being gay? No, I'm not ashamed of being gay. However, I do doubt my strength to overcome the harassment if I were confronted directly. It's bound to happen. What will I say? I keep all of my co-workers at arm's length. During lunchtime conversations, I spend a lot of energy keeping me out of the spotlight. I'm always on guard for questions about whom I might be dating. Ready for a quick, funny response. Turning the focus back to those around me. Away from me. But the dating questions never come. Only once did a coworker ask—years ago when I first started working at the school. So, I told her. I told her the truth. I told her about my partner, my girlfriend. I asked her not to tell anyone. Keep it between us, I said. She didn't make any promises. No one has asked me since.

I am an aunt to eight nieces and one nephew. To my nieces and nephew, I am the fun aunt because when I visit, they get my undivided attention. I do not have my own children to tend to, just my dog and cat. With the oldest niece just turning twelve, questions are starting to arise about why I am not married. So, I tell them that I don't want to get married. My "friend" and I are happy living together. My mom said I should say, "Two women can't get married." But I said that wasn't true. I have gay friends who are married. My siblings all seem to be at different stages of understanding and accepting. Sometimes I find myself getting tongue-tied when they ask me questions. Why do I still feel like a monkey in a cage at a zoo—people watching me in amazement?

I am a lesbian. I have a wonderful set of friends, just a handful of close friends. I notice I am less introverted with my close friends. I have a lot to say when I am around them. I do not have to be on guard, afraid I might say something that would cause people to whisper and wonder. I don't have to filter my conversations, and I don't have to worry about what pronouns I use.

I am a daughter. To my parents, I am the youngest of four children. They are proud of many of my life accomplishments—teaching, being a good aunt, my good health, my nice home in a good area, many of my morals, visiting with them fairly often. But the lesbian "side," well, that's the elephant in the room that keeps getting sidestepped. I know they don't approve. That's their biggest disappointment about me.

I'm a spouse. I met my partner through mutual friends nine years ago while I was still living in Columbia, Missouri. She was living two hours away. Before meeting her, I was planning to move, perhaps to the city she lived in with the hope of finding a job sometime the following summer. After applying to many schools in that area, I knew God had a plan for me with my girlfriend when I got a job within a ten-minute drive from her home. After we met, everything started falling into place; everything just seemed easier. How could God NOT be playing a role in this? My partner asks, when I reach those pearly gates of Heaven, what is the worst thing God can say about me being gay? Nothing. I have done as God told me. I loved another human being unconditionally—that person just happened to be another woman.

Most important, I am a child of God. I know that now. God sees all sides of me. God sees me struggle, celebrate, accept, love, and pray about who I am. God put me on earth for many reasons, and I know one of them included being gay and celebrating my differences. I see being gay as a gift now, not a curse. Even though others see me in a different light, my faith community helps me to nourish my spirituality. I have a long way to go with God and my spirituality—a lot of learning to take in, a lot of love to discover, and a lot of patience to find. Although I still hear about protesters carrying "God hates…" signs, I find myself mentally changing the word *hate* to "love," because I know that is what God is all about. It is that simple. God does not hate. God is love. That's it. So, I am loved. God is that grandparent who has unconditional love to give. And I am the child that not only gets to receive that love, but I also get to give that love freely.

My Story

Margaret Kastigar

Margaret is dedicated to serving the poor and is devoted to her family and friends. She enjoys bike riding and is a closeted listener to Christian music.

I was born and raised in a Catholic family, with seven brothers and sisters. I have aunts who were nuns, two uncles who were priests, and one brother who has been a diocesan priest for more than twenty-five years. I went to Catholic grade school, high school, and a Jesuit university for my undergraduate studies. The Catholic tradition is ingrained in me. We didn't always buy the whole enchilada, but we could recite chapter and verse. There were disagreements, arguments, and discussions about papal edicts, bishops' letters, and homilies. We were raised fully in the Catholic tradition.

In about 1978, my uncle, who had been a priest more than twenty-seven years came by and announced to my parents (subsequently it oozed down to us) that he was leaving the priesthood to marry. He was, and is still, my favorite uncle. He was always at our home at least twice a week for dinner, helping dad with projects or taking us kids to the park, so that my parents could have a few minutes of much needed adult time.

I remember my parents' responses. They were so surprised and hurt. He had kept this huge secret to himself for quite some time. I remember perceiving that the hurt and surprise were not so much about his leaving the priesthood, but about leaving them out of this process in his life. His wife is a lovely lady and a wonderful addition to the family, though we certainly resented her initially, not for taking him from the church, but from *our* regular visits.

Though I questioned my sexual orientation as early as high school and certainly through college, I don't recall rejecting the Catholic faith through that time. Perhaps that seems a contradiction, but it was so ingrained in me that I just didn't. I questioned the teachings and the policies, and I still do, but I cannot seem to reject it. I continued to attend Mass regularly through high school (under my parents' roof) and even when away at college, enjoying the energy and charism of a university-based faith community. While an undergraduate, I remember seeking counsel from a Jesuit priest about my feelings about women. My memory of his response is, "at the very worst, you're bisexual."

I had my first lesbian relationship when I was at the end of my graduate program. I had moved out of my parents' home and was not particularly active in church at the time.

During this relationship, I did explore Dignity. I was trying to "come out" to my family, my peers, and myself. Trying to figure out what it really meant to identify as a lesbian and Catholic, and Dignity did help with that. I remember feeling very supported and graced to find a church where this "difference" that I was trying to name, define, and fit into my life was embraced openly, within the comfort and familiarity of my childhood faith.

I stayed with that faith community for some time, enjoying the familiarity of worship and gospel, though the Dignity chapter I was involved in had its own issues, difficulties, and biases, as sometimes happens, and I struggled with those. Eventually, I stopped going to Dignity and stayed away from church for several years. Never, though, did I reject or negate it. I continued to attend church for family functions or at others' request. I began feeling somewhat "out of the loop," but I could always rely on a familiarity with the basic rituals from childhood. I knew when to get up, sit down, kneel, what prayer to say. It's amazing how that comes back to you like yesterday!

A few years later, God called me back. Better stated, I began to listen to God's call for me to return. My friend Joan and I started "church shopping." We'd attend a different service every Sunday and then meet our partners afterwards for breakfast and discussion. I'm not even sure how the process began, but we went to many wonderful services of various faiths and in different areas of town, and we both ended up choosing different churches (both Catholic parishes) at the end of the process. I attended my new parish regularly for several years and still consider it my "parish," though my ongoing attendance is not weekly.

The Catholic Church is still where I go when I'm lost. It's not my first home, but I compare it to going to my mother's home. I'm comfortable there. It's familiar. I know where she keeps the silverware, snacks, and soda pop, and I'll help myself. But I don't want to move back in.

When I describe myself, I include Catholic. I'm Catholic, middle-aged, lesbian. I went to my aunt's funeral last spring, and my uncle preached his very Catholic homily. At first, I thought, "good grief, he's so hard-line!" Then I remembered. We put such store in our faith and get such comfort from it. It is where we go when we are lost. He's burying his sister, his only remaining sibling! He's torn to the core, and he goes to the basics. God is love. Our faith carries us through. The church is our mainstay.

Even when the hierarchy of the church rejects us, the people of the church—God and His people—embrace our humanness, our brokenness, our "alike-ness."

God continues to call us. Again and again.

Lesbian Catholic

Jo Soske

Jo has a saltwater soul and, in retirement, she has returned to her beloved sea. Living on island time, she spends her days volunteering as a pastoral assistant at the hospital, teaching Spanish to senior citizens, teaching Spanish-language CCE, and occasionally writing. She spends her evenings walking on the beach with her partner of eighteen years and their Brittany spaniel.

I have struggled with how to begin this narrative because I know that the use of labels can conjure up stereotypes. For some Catholics, if I say that I am a lesbian, they will immediately begin to think in terms of rampant sexual promiscuity. In fact, the word lesbian tells them no more about my sexual behavior than the word heterosexual tells me about theirs. Even if I were to say that I am a lesbian with a life partner, I have given them very limited information. It may be that I enjoy a vibrant, loving sexual life, or it may be that I live in committed celibacy, as many heterosexual couples choose to do for numerous reasons, including disability. On the other hand for some lesbians, particularly lesbian feminists, the word Catholic will conjure up visions of blind submission to patriarchy or even violent physical attacks against women attempting to enter abortion clinics. In fact, the word Catholic tells almost nothing about my political beliefs. People in the Catholic Church range from the traditionalist members of Opus Dei to those who believe in the principles of liberation theology. I am neither politically conservative nor promiscuous. Having said that, I will begin this account in the most logical way. I am a lesbian Catholic, and it has taken me years to come to the personal understanding that those two descriptions can co-exist. The dilemma presented by being both Catholic and lesbian led to years of effort to deny one or the other of these two essential aspects of my identity. Today, though, I understand these terms to involve neither contradiction nor sin.

Like many homosexuals, I passed through years of inner struggle before coming to terms with my sexual identity. The echoes of "difference" reverberated through childhood, as much for my passionate interest in religion—my family was decidedly secular—as for my strong emotional attachments to other girls. It took only a couple of experiences with being called that most dreaded of all words, "queer," to convince me that I should conform to the norm and make every effort to hide the truth from everybody, including me.

Adolescence often brings a season of turmoil and unrest, and there were numerous occasions on which I began, once again, to suspect that I was somehow different from my friends. As a teenager, I was religious and also outspoken and rebellious. I became involved with the women's movement in 1970, when I was sixteen years old. I wrote a few articles for a feminist newspaper, *Fifty-One Percent*—one of the first in the country. Those were invigorating times. We were filled with hope and excitement. We were standing on the threshold of a new dawn. Girls and women were going to share fully in the countless opportunities already available to boys and men. I was fascinated to hear that there was a lesbian presence in the women's movement. But in the end, I was more frightened than I was fascinated and more compliant than I was rebellious. I never investigated; instead, I doubled my efforts to appear normal, and I was seldom without a boyfriend. But with each passing year it became clearer to me that I had absolutely no interest in marrying.

Like many young people during the late '60s and early '70s, I was interested in building a better world, a world in which love would flourish and war and poverty would end. I strongly considered entering the Peace Corps, but I was more strongly drawn to a life where spiritual values were at the core. I was one of those kids blessed by the presence of older women in my life who served as mentors. Two women, in particular, shaped the direction of my life when I was young. One was the editor and publisher of *Fifty-One Percent*. She was my junior year English teacher, an outspoken antiwar feminist. To this day, I have never had a better teacher. Everything about her life shouted "...and justice for all." The other woman was a sister in the order of St. Joseph of Carondelet. She was of Mexican descent and an advocate of activism. She participated in the California grape boycott and marched with Cesar Chavez. Her birthday was on the feast day of Our Lady of Guadalupe, and she was my godmother. I wanted very much to live a life that emulated these two strong women and made a difference in the world.

I decided to enter the convent, with hopes of eventually being sent to Guatemala. The religious life seemed like the perfect fit since God and the church were two of the most important relationships in my life. I was in complete denial about my lesbianism and the role that it would play in shaping these two relationships. So I left Los Angeles, where I had grown up, and entered a religious community in Oklahoma City. My denial was soon to be challenged. Early in my novitiate, I fell deeply, profoundly in love with another novice. I recognized the feelings, but I refused to believe that they were a reflection of my sexual identity. I assumed that these romantic feelings were about this one particular woman, and they would pass. I was extremely confused. I loved religious life, I wanted to make promises, and I was also very much in love with a woman.

One Saturday, I attempted to discuss these feelings during confession. Many sisters from my community were waiting in line, outside the confessional, for their opportunity to participate in the sacrament. The priest began to yell at me. He told me that I was sick. I wanted to run and hide. I was deeply humiliated. Walking out of that confessional was one of the harder things that I have done. The leaders of our community recognized the feelings that the other novice and I had for one another. They warned us against the dangers of "particular friendship" and advised us to talk to one another only in community. Neither my particular friend nor I heeded the warnings. We sought out every possible opportunity to spend time together.

Eventually, I was asked to leave the convent. Apparently, the mother general and novice mistress had a sense that these were transitory feelings for my friend, but they were a reflection of my sexual identity. She was allowed to stay. I was devastated. I had to leave both a life that I loved and a woman that I loved. I was terrified that this might mean that I was gay. My understanding of homosexuality at that time was pretty simple: abnormal and sinful. This was not the life that I wanted. Upon leaving the convent, I worked harder than ever to maintain my comfortable state of denial, but it was more difficult. Dishonesty is corrosive. It erodes self-respect, and with each new lie, the next lie becomes both easier and more destructive. I reached for a crutch often used by those who suffer from internalized homophobia, substance abuse.

Substance abuse was not new to my life: the seeds of addiction had been planted generations earlier on both the Irish/English side of my family and the Polish/German side. But after being asked to leave the convent, I traveled down that road at an alarmingly rapid rate. I consumed my substance of choice in large quantities, and I clung to the hope that I was "normal," that is, heterosexual. As a result, within months of leaving the convent, I became pregnant. I was stunned to find out that I was pregnant, because I had acted impulsively in a substance-induced haze. But I have never regretted the pregnancy or the child to whom I gave birth. I believe in the spiritual axiom that some of our greatest blessings come out of periods of great pain. That is certainly the case where my son is concerned.

Even so, finding out that I was going to have a child only added to my confusion. What was I to do? Thanks to the sage advice of a beloved friend, Kathy, who later became my baby's godmother, I spared my son, his father, and myself the pain of a loveless marriage. I did not want his father as a life partner, but I very much wanted my son. That decision, though, and subsequent decisions made by his father, meant that my son grew up without the love and guidance of a father, and his father lived his life without the love and joy of a son. In seeking to deceive myself, I had brought pain into the lives of others.

Unfortunately, during the weeks before I realized that I was pregnant, I had engaged in periods of heavy substance use. And truth be told, I continued some use after I knew that I was pregnant. With concern in my heart, I went to Mass every Sunday, and I sat next to a stained glass window depicting St. Anne, Mary's mother. I thought a lot about motherhood. I prayed and asked God to allow my son to be born healthy, and I promised to raise him in the Catholic Church.

My prayers were answered on a cold January day, when I gave birth to a beautiful, healthy 7 lb. 6 1/2 oz. boy, Jon Dylan. After Jon's birth, I worked, returned to the university, set about keeping my promise to raise him in the church, and continued to use my substance of choice while denying my sexual identity. Unfortunately for my son, I was slipping further into addiction as I fought to maintain my denial.

My first certified teaching job was in a Catholic school. I enjoyed the job, and I loved my students. I felt a true sense of mission teaching there. Each Sunday, my son and I attended Mass. My life was very Catholic. But there was a nagging sensation that something wasn't right, and the substance abuse continued, particularly on weekends. From time to time my denial would be threatened. I would feel an attraction to another woman or a deep emotional, almost romantic, attachment to a friend. Generally, the recipients of these feelings were women who were safe, that is, happily married or committed to a celibate religious life. Thus, I never had to fully acknowledge the feelings.

When Jon was four years old, however, my denial ended abruptly. I made a new friend, and once again, I fell in love with a woman. She was heterosexual, and her love for me was not the same as mine for her, but we became life-long friends, and we loved one another until the day that she died. The experience of falling in love with her opened my eyes. I could no longer tell myself that it was a fluke or that it was due to circumstances. It was now clear to me, I loved her romantically because I was a lesbian. I began to say the words aloud, "I am a lesbian." The freedom and liberation that came with those words was indescribable. Only one other time in my life would words bring a similar sense of freedom. Every chance I got, I repeated the words, "I am a lesbian." They fit, and I set out to find other women like myself.

It was a point of no return. Never again would I return to the denial of the past, nor would I wish to. But there were many places in which it was not safe to say those words, "I am a lesbian." I lived in a very conservative state, and I was often employed in school settings. If the truth were known about my life, I could have lost my job. I even feared losing my child. I lived my life with one foot out of the closet and the other in the closet. The church was certainly one of those places where it did not feel safe to speak out about my lesbianism.

Within six months of coming out, I was able to admit that I had a problem with substance abuse, and I sought help. I went to my priest, who shared my problem, and he sent me to a twelve-step program. I no longer needed the crutch of a substance to help me bury my identity. After recognizing my lesbianism, I was able to recognize my chemical dependence. With God's help, I got sober. In my twelve-step program, they told me that in order to recover, I had to live a life of rigorous honesty. Rigorous honesty can present difficulties for a lesbian who works in education and lives in the Midwest. This was even more true in 1982, when I got sober. But I determined to be as honest and open as I possibly could. I was completely out with all of my family members. Unlike many gays, I have always enjoyed the blessing of a family that is wonderfully supportive. I also chose to have only close friends with whom I could be fully honest. And in the work environment, I made a conscious decision always to find at least one person with whom I could be completely and fully out. Thus, the closet door never entirely closed.

The church continued to be very important to me. There too, I found people with whom I could be honest. I was involved with the Catholic peace movement through Pax Christi, and my son and I spent a lot of time at a Benedictine convent called the Peace House, where the nuns knew that I was a lesbian. We rallied for peace on the steps of the Oklahoma City Federal Building, never dreaming that it would one day be the site of terrible death and destruction. But when my denial about my sexual identity ended, my problems with the church as an institution began. I continued to attend Mass with my son, though less regularly than previously. My involvement with the Peace House slowly came to an end. I did see to it that my son attended Catholic religious instruction, made his First Communion, and even attended Catholic school for a couple of years.

But I had a love-hate relationship with the church. Attending Mass gave me the same sense of spiritual connection that it always had, but I saw the church as an oppressive, patriarchal institution that told me that I was sinful for being who I am. Much of the time, I felt alienated from, and angry with, the church. I thought, from time to time, about leaving it. I often felt that I was living a double life. I was finally free from living one lie, only to find myself living another one. How could I be both a practicing Catholic and a lesbian? How could I be a lesbian and do God's will at the same time?

In the end, it was a twelve-step program, not the church, that gave me the peace of mind and acceptance that I needed about my sexual identity. In the basic text of one twelve-step program, it says, "We found that God does not make too hard terms with those who seek Him (sic). To us the Realm of Spirit is broad, roomy, all-inclusive; never exclusive or forbidding to those who earnestly seek. It is open, we believe, to all men (sic)." I equated this very strongly with the statement in the documents of Vatican II that says "...any movement toward goodness is a movement toward God." Reflecting on these two statements gave me a great sense of peace, and I came to believe that God would not have created me a lesbian and then rejected me for being one. Though I found internal peace about my sexual identity, my difficulties with the church and society at large were not resolved.

All of this, I believe, had far-reaching consequences for my son. He was raised with mixed messages and a double ethic. On one hand, I told him that honesty was important and should be valued at all times. On the other hand, I warned him against saying too much about "Mom's sexual preference" outside of the family. There were people in society who did not understand, and it might cause problems for him with his friends at school and church, and for me on the job. This is an unfair and heavy burden to ask a child to carry. I deeply regret this, but I couldn't see any way around it without lying to him, and I found that alternative to be unacceptable. Family secrets create shame and sick families.

The church teaches that gays and lesbians must remain sexually abstinent. I have no intention of debating that teaching, but I do want to make two points with respect to it. First, it is a matter of my personal, private conscience whether or not I believe that being in a faithful, committed relationship with a same-sex partner is right. Secondly, in calling on gays and lesbians to be celibate, the hierarchy of the church has set a standard for the homosexual community that they themselves have yet to meet. For years, I was angry with the church for what I perceived to be unjust treatment of homosexuals and women, and as a result, I tried very hard to leave the Catholic Church without ever fully achieving it. Let there be no mistake, I continue to perceive the church to be unjust to women and homosexuals. The difference is, I have ceased trying to leave. I now believe that the church belongs as much to those who think as I do as it does to those who perpetuate the oppression.

Shortly before my son left for college, I met a beautiful, talented, spiritual woman. She was a Lutheran, and I was a struggling Catholic. We talked about attending church together, and after Jon left, we began visiting churches. We finally settled on an Episcopal Church where the priest was an old and dear friend of mine. It seemed the perfect fit. I was certainly more comfortable with Episcopalian views than with Roman Catholic views. Not only did they ordain women, they were openly discussing the possibility of ordaining gays and blessing same-sex unions.

I participated in the Episcopal Church for nine years, though not exclusively. I could never seem to refrain completely from returning to an occasional Catholic Mass. In spite of this, my involvement in the Episcopal Church deepened, and I even believed that I might have a vocation to the deaconate. After all, I had once felt called to religious life… wouldn't it be a natural progression?

But, during my time in the Episcopal Church, I was often restless and discontented with the progress that was being made. Even though the Episcopal Church was taking great strides forward while the Catholic Church seemed to being moving backward, I felt that Episcopalians should be moving more quickly to include homosexuals fully in the life of the church. I openly voiced these opinions, speaking and writing to the bishop more than once. He seemed to listen deeply, and in the end he was a deciding vote for the ordination of Bishop Eugene Robinson, the first openly gay Episcopal bishop.

At the end of 2002, I was very involved in the Episcopal Church. Among many other activities, I was attending Education for Ministry (EFM), a theology course related to ministry. Though I had encountered several roadblocks, the deaconate was very much on my mind. Being fluent in Spanish, I was deeply interested in Hispanic ministry. Unbeknown to me, I was about to enter a period of loss thus far unparalleled in my life, throughout which God's presence was to be very active, at times subtly, at times almost tangibly. And very slowly, without giving it much thought, the Catholic Church would once again be woven into the tapestry of my life.

In addition to teaching full time, I had a small private counseling practice. Ninety-five percent of my clients were lesbians, many dealing with issues related to homophobia. In the fall of 2002, after thirteen years of practice, I decided, rather suddenly, and without clearly defined reasons, that I wanted to close my practice. I did so on December 31, 2002. Two weeks later, doctors discovered spots on my mother's liver, adrenal glands, and lung. She was scheduled to have a biopsy in Torrance, California.

Two days before my mother was to have her biopsy, I was driving to work on a cold Oklahoma morning. My intention was to wait for the results of the biopsy and then determine when I should go to California. That morning, as I drove to school, I felt a very sudden and very strong presence in the car with me. It was as if God, my deceased grandmother, and my deceased aunt were there with me. I could almost touch them. I felt that they were telling me not to go to school that day, but rather to go immediately to California. Moreover, I felt that they were telling me very clearly that, if I did not do so, I would regret it for the remainder of my life. I am not a person known for acting spontaneously. Neither was I one to miss work. But that particular morning I listened to the feelings. I went to school; made arrangements to take leave; sent a quick e-mail to my sisters and Jon telling them what I was about to do; called my partner, Karen, to say goodbye; and left for California. I left Oklahoma, in my truck, at 10:30 a.m. on a Monday morning, and I arrived in Los Angeles at 5:30 p.m. on Tuesday.

My mother was not happy to see me—it concerned her that I had driven that long distance alone, and she felt that my visit was premature. But when I said, "Mom, we are going to go together in the morning to find out what it is that we are facing," she softened. And together we went.

At the hospital, my mother and I met with her doctor, to receive and impart information. I then went to the waiting room, with my father, to await the conclusion of the biopsy. And while I waited, I read my next lesson of Episcopalian theology. As I studied, I heard them call "code blue" on the intercom system. I thought, almost passively, "Oh, somebody has coded," followed quickly by, "It's my mother. My mother has coded." And, in fact, she had. As I saw them rush her from the room, toward emergency, performing CPR, I knew why it was that I had had to come. My father was in shock, completely unable to respond to the doctor's questions about her health history. With hands shaking, I called my siblings and my son, as the doctors worked to revive my mother. And revive her they did. This was to be only the first day of a journey that would last seven and a half months and end in her death. She was in intensive care and then on the cardiac unit for five days. I sat with her during much of that time. At some point, I once again picked up my theology course, and I re-read the last line that I had underlined, just before hearing the words, "code blue." It said, "If you listen to my words, I will be with you." I found that to be very true. God was very much with me during those difficult months.

Though I was living in Oklahoma, I traveled to California six or seven times between late January and October of 2003. Most trips were made by a combination of train and car.

My life was very fragmented, and I was deeply sad and profoundly exhausted. During the times that I was in Oklahoma, I continued my high level of involvement in the Episcopal Church. However, during my times in California, I never attended the Episcopal Church. Instead, I felt drawn to attend Catholic Mass. Once or twice, I attended with my father, but more often I felt the desire to go alone to Our Lady of Guadalupe Church, where I had been baptized. On one of my trips to California, I bought a rosary at the train station in New Mexico. I didn't actually pray the rosary, but I held it during my morning meditation, and it brought me much-needed comfort.

In June of that same year, suddenly, without warning, my friend, for whom my love had freed me to say the words, "I am a lesbian," died of an unexpected complication of MS. We had remained close for more than twenty years—she having lived in Peru working with liberation theologians, and I a Spanish teacher; both of us engaging in long phone conversations, in Spanish, in which we solved the problems of the world. I had spoken to her only days earlier, and then she was gone. How is it that life can be so unpredictable, so fleeting?

The summer of 2003 was the summer of the Episcopal General Convention. This was to be the year that I had longed for, the year in which homosexuals would be included fully in the life of the church. Yet, at times, I actually forgot that the convention was taking place. On the day that the vote was taken in favor of the ordination of Bishop Robinson, I learned about it on the Internet; my dying mother was sleeping in the next room. I felt no joy, no elation. This long-awaited moment came and passed, barely noticed by me.

It embarrasses me to say that I am a phobic flier. Moreover, the motion of flying makes me intensely ill. I have two sisters who suffer from the same malady. It is an understatement to say that I will generally go to any lengths to avoid flying, so intense is my aversion. On the Saturday morning of Labor Day weekend, 2003, I was in Oklahoma, having returned home to get things prepared for the start of the new school year, with the intention of later returning to California to be with my mother. That Saturday morning, after my morning meditation, I said to my partner, Karen, "I feel that I should go to California today to see my mother. Please call to see if we can get a flight." Karen was absolutely dumbfounded. During the more than ten years we had spent together, I had never flown anywhere. She didn't believe that I was serious, but she called nonetheless. Not only were there seats available, on a flight leaving in less than two hours, but the round trip cost was under $350 per person. She booked the flight. I had a picture of our Lady of Guadalupe, whose feast day I regularly celebrated. That's the only thing that I remember taking with me. I held it on my lap, and whenever I felt anxious or nauseated, I looked at it and prayed. Looking at that picture and praying accomplished something for me that therapy, books, tapes, and a fear-of-flying course had not. Without incident or illness, I flew to California and spent the weekend with my mother. She died nine days later, early on a September morning, with my sister, Jessica, by her side. We eulogized my mother at a park overlooking the Pacific Ocean, where we released butterflies on October 3, and we buried her at sea on October 4. There was no better date than the feast of St. Francis to say goodbye to my mother, a life-long ecologist and guardian of injured animals. Of our mother's death my sister wrote that you can know it is coming, you can see it coming, you can begin preparing yourself for it, yet when it happens, it is still like being hit by a train. And thus it was.

As is true for many people, I found the first holidays following my mother's death to be very difficult. In November Karen, Linda (a friend from my convent days), and I drove to Galveston Island. Jon flew down from Toronto, where he was a graduate student, and we spent Thanksgiving together. I wanted to be near the ocean, and I have always loved Galveston, where I now live during part of the year. While we were there, I chose not to attend one of the lovely Episcopal churches on the island, but rather to go to Catholic Mass. The weekend passed rather peacefully.

Christmas proved to be much more difficult. When Christmas Eve arrived that year, I chose to spend it alone. First I talked on the phone to an older cousin. We talked about my mother and his mother and our grandmother. Then, I went to Catholic Mass. As I thought of my mother, the sadness was overwhelming, and it was only in kneeling to light a candle and pray for my sisters, who I knew to be having a similar experience, that I felt some peace. The months of travel, sleepless nights, and caretaking had taken their toll on me physically and emotionally. I was experiencing some health problems, and I longed for summer when there would be time to rest, remember, and grieve. But that would not come to pass.

In spite of my exhaustion, I made yet another trip to California during spring break, this one, though, for a joyous occasion. Though I had given the general convention and its aftermath little heed, the results had a profound effect on my life. In March of 2004, Karen and I traveled to Grace Cathedral in San Francisco, where ten years of shared commitment, based on spiritual principles, were blessed by an Episcopalian priest. This is something that the Catholic Church may never afford its gay and lesbian faithful. March 17, 2004, was one of the best days of my entire life. I remember everything about it. There before God, the priest, my sister Jessica, and two witnesses, we were able to say what we had known to be true for more than a decade. The priest gave a very powerful message, and I was particularly touched when he spoke of "...those of us who come from Catholic and Anglican traditions...." He was speaking to me. I shall forever be indebted to the Episcopal Church for that day.

I returned to Oklahoma longing for the restful days of summer, but a week before school ended, I found myself with physical custody, and later temporary guardianship, of two great-nieces. Though I loved them very much, nothing in my previous experience as a mother, a teacher, or a counselor had prepared me for the energy, patience, and financial commitment that it takes to parent two traumatized girls, one teen and one pre-teen. Still, they needed to be protected, and I was available to do so. They lived with me for four-teen months. Just as I knew that the solution for substance abuse, grief, and most of life's challenges is a strong spiritual foundation, I believed also that it was one of the solutions for trauma. And I set about to provide them with that. Their grandmother, my sister-in-law, had had them baptized in the Evangelical Lutheran Church of America (ELCA) in infancy. The Episcopal Church, which is in full communion with ELCA Lutherans, made perfect sense. Either Karen or I or both took them to church every week and, together, we prepared them to make their First Communion in the Episcopal Church. However, I also enrolled the youngest girl in Catholic Religious Education (RE) and the older girl in a Catholic youth group. The reasoning I gave myself was that the Catholic church was closer to our house, and they would have a chance to make friends in their own neighborhood. Was it possible that I wanted them to have a connection with the parish where I once taught and Jon once attended school?

One Wednesday evening, I picked up the youngest girl, Marisa, following RE. She ran to the truck excitedly and said, "I want to be Catholic when I grow up." I said, "I can understand that Marisa, but it's a big commitment, and there will be things you must learn about the Catholic Church."

"Like what?" She asked.

"Uh, well, hum. Did you know that women can't be priests in the Catholic Church?" I asked.

She gasped, "You're kidding! That's just wrong! That's, well that's—that's like racism."

"We call it sexism, Marisa."

"Really?" She asked, and then after a while she added, "Why don't you call it genderism?"

In spite of wonderful moments like that, at age fifty, I had no real desire to raise two girls to adulthood. After only a few months, the goal became reunification with their birth mother, once she could accumulate enough months of sobriety and financial resources to properly care for them.

Karen and I do not live in the same house. She lives next door. But she shared in every aspect of caring for the girls. I realize now that we did an excellent job of parenting, under very difficult circumstances. During the time that the girls were with us, we traveled extensively, went on picnics, rode bicycles, played games, and celebrated holidays. We attended their school functions, and we helped them with homework. There were times of great joy amid times of great stress. There were also more times of sorrow. My sister, Julie, was the first of my sisters to be diagnosed with a serious auto-immune disease. Less than four months later, in April, there was more sadness. Within a period of two weeks, there were three deaths. First, a man who had been my grand-sponsor in a twelve-step program for more than twenty years died. Then, I received a brief note telling me that a cousin had passed. The third death, though, resulted in a depth of grief that I am still at a loss to explain.

Kathy, my son's godmother, my comadre, my friend of more than thirty years, died from complications related to rheumatoid arthritis. Even now, I am unable to write about her death without crying. Few people are blessed to have a friend of the type that Kathy was for me. We unfailingly shared our truths, even difficult truths. She loved me unconditionally. We could go months without talking, yet each phone conversation was as though we had never been apart. She often ended by saying, "I love you Jo Soske," and I knew with every inch of my being that she was telling the truth. Her death was one of the great losses of my life.

Though Kathy had left the church many years earlier, a priest who had known her since she was a teenager presided at her services. He gave what may have been the most beautiful homily I have ever heard. He spoke of the great human need for a home and how we often find that home in someone's heart. I had a home in Kathy's heart, and she will always have one in mine.

Soon after Kathy's death, I had a dream in which my mother appeared as she had been in life. In the dream, she told me to return to the Catholic Church.

Upon awakening, I immediately discounted the dream. My mother was not Catholic, and she had no investment in the Catholic Church. She found her spiritual connection through nature.

Three months after Kathy died, after more than a year of counseling, legal challenges, and setbacks, we finally reached our goal for the girls. On July 28, 2005, the judge awarded physical and residential custody to their mother, and the girls moved fully into her apartment. The following day was my fifty-first birthday. It was to be a birthday like none other.

Both of my sisters had sent me gifts the week before my birthday, but on the actual day of my birth, I received no phone calls, cards, or e-mails from friends. Nor did I hear from my son, the girls, their mother, or any other family member, except my father. For some unknown reason, that year, everybody forgot. Perhaps at age fifty-one, that should not have seemed very important, but it did. I slipped into a deep, almost paralyzing sadness. And as has been my custom for many years, I went to a twelve-step meeting. I shared honestly, though somewhat incoherently, about my feelings. But for perhaps the first time since I've been in the program, I received little consolation or spiritual insight. A long-time program friend, whom I greatly respect, pointed out to me that I was wallowing in self-pity. She was, of course, correct. But it was more than that, much more. I was weary to the bone. And without giving it any forethought, I found myself sitting alone in a dark Catholic church. I wasn't praying, I wasn't even thinking. I was simply sitting there and perhaps occasionally crying. I don't know how long I was there before going home for the evening, but I felt some peace, so I returned the following day. For three days, I went to the church and sat, not measuring time, not questioning my reasons for being there. Without warning and without asking permission, it had arrived—my summer of grief.

One hot August day, less than a month after the time spent sitting in the darkened church, I was operating a children's booth at a festival to raise money for an Hispanic Episcopal parish. It was my fourth year to do so. But this particular year, I had decided to leave early to attend my friend's daughter's wedding. It was to be celebrated in Spanish, at a nearby Catholic church. So, leaving my booth behind, I drove from an Episcopal parish to a Catholic parish.

When I entered the church, I was somewhat surprised to see all of the living sisters from the religious community that I had joined more than thirty years earlier. I sat with them during the wedding mass, and I began to ask myself, "What is it? Why do I feel so much more at home and so much more at peace in this Mass, in this church with which I have so many profound and honest disagreements? What is here?" There were no logical answers. There are no logical answers. Spirituality is not about logic.

At the end of the service, the bride and groom knelt before a statue of Our Lady of Guadalupe and placed flowers at her feet. A soloist began to sing *Ave Maria,* and the tears began to roll down my cheeks. I knew in the innermost depths of my being that I was home, and I would no longer be able to stay away. I was, in fact, being called to be who I am, a lesbian Catholic. At long last, both of those words, lesbian and Catholic, brought freedom. The struggle was over. I didn't have to know why, I didn't have to have a logical explanation, I only had to rest in the knowing that I am as Catholic as I am lesbian and as lesbian as I am Catholic.

Reflections...

At the Center—Fear and Courage

Many of the women I have met during my lesbian and gay ministry are vulnerable because of the hostility they have experienced from our church and our culture. They are criticized or condemned because all too frequently others see them as engaging in deviant sexual activity. Heterosexuals have often been fixated on this—as though being gay is only about having sex. But it is much deeper than that. As we see so clearly in Jo's writing, it is really all about identity. It is about who am I at my core, the center of my being. It is as deep as questions about who I am as a woman or a man.

When moralists judge persons because of their orientation, it cuts into this identity center within them. It is like being called mean and ugly names. It *is* being called names. It is taking all that I think is dirty and sinful and hurling it at someone. It hurts deeply, cuts and bruises the personality and soul of the person herself.

Our group writes about who we are at our center core. We want to describe our experiences, our fears, our hopes, our dreams, and values. But some of our women have dropped out. I can understand that. They can't write because of the fear—no one knows who they truly are. They might or would be rejected if family and friends knew. It is not safe to be out: "I can be rejected, ostracized, criticized, judged, called names, have things thrown at me, be beaten, be murdered, lose my home, lose my loved one, lose custody of my children." As Charlotte says, "I'm very careful about not causing waves, bringing attention to myself." I listen to the despair, the pain, and sadness in their voices.

"I come to the meeting because I see myself as a spiritual person. I belong to a church. I love this church. It is family. It is home," Jessica tells the group. In saying this, she echoes Margaret. And Jessica continues, "The church condemns me. Some of the parishioners I go to church with don't accept me. They look down their hypocritical noses at me. If I question myself too deeply, I might have to leave. I will feel hurt again." Jessica is just out of college. She should be filled with hope and promise. Although she is at a more mature stage of her life, Kasey expresses a similar thought: this is home and no longer home.

Joan reads her story aloud to us and says, "When I read what I have written, I cry, again. This is something I wrote a year ago, yet I cry again. My partner across the room from me cries, too. She has not heard me read this all the way through before." The room is quiet. We can hear the cat downstairs crying because she wants to be up here with us.

The crying of the cat gives sound to a silent cry that is deep in our own hearts.

One woman can't write about her life because it is too complicated. Isn't life like that? Complicated? Her husband doesn't want to be "outed." So her life is silenced, too.

On this cloudy March Sunday, we pray about the Good Shepherd. We feel hopeful that the shepherd in the reading reaches out to the lost sheep. I reflect with the group, "Also within us there can be lost parts. We need all of ourselves to be whole and to seek wholeness. We can't leave parts of ourselves in the dark, in the silence."

I see the beauty of the women's stories. I want desperately for others to hear them. Yet some are fearful. I, too, feel fearful. I fear the project might be falling apart because of their fear. I would like to talk about my fears, but I don't express them. I wish I could say to them, "I would like to write about your fears, but I can't do it the way you can. You are the voices that can talk about this. I can only quote you."

Fear rules all of our lives more than we realize and more than we would like to admit. I think those who live with oppression know about this fear. They know more than anyone else how much we need each other, we influence each other, we desperately need to be loved and accepted. Our fears tell us about who we are as a society. Fear holds up a mirror. We look into it, and we don't like what we see. We project our fears onto others. We begin to fear them. We express this fear as hatred.

I have to face my own fear. Can I be with these women as an advocate? It feels like the climate in our church has become less hospitable each year since I started in this ministry. I fear this project is falling apart—everything feels so vulnerable, so fragile. I want these stories to be told. I am beginning to doubt that this can happen. I only hope that together we can find healing and, courageously, move beyond fear.

TRUSTING

*No soul is desolate as long as there is a human being
for whom it can feel trust and reverence.*

— *George Eliot*

Recollections . . .

Dreamscape

At our next meeting together, I share a dream with the group, using it as our opening reflection. I think it is related to who we are and what we do when we gather.

I made a CD of a couple of songs I had planned to use. I go over to the church to get it. I had left it in the sacristy. I enter the sacristy, and I see the sound system and other CDs, but not mine.

While I am in the sacristy I see people walking around getting ready for Mass. I am afraid I might see the pastor. I don't want to meet up with him. I don't know what to say to him. He is so intimidating, and he has been judgmental of me and my ministry in the past. Even though there are others all around me, I feel alone. No one seems to notice me, or even to see me.

I look out into the church. It is lighted up, and everyone is there ready for Mass to begin. The church is large and oval-shaped, very modern, with blonde pews that match the wood of the altar. I walk into the church.

I am thinking that I will go find a place and stay for Mass. But I find a stairway that leads me to the basement. Everything is grey, and it is large and cavernous down here. One large area, made of stone and concrete, has two towers in it. I notice that the windows in the towers are made of stained glass. I am looking at them from the outside. The ground looks like a garden with rich, dark soil, but no grass or flowers. There are some copper ironwork spirals that surround this space. I look up and see dark, open space from here. I am amazed at all there is here under the church.

The floor of the basement is soil, and while I walk around in it, my beige pumps do not get dirty. I walk around from one side to the other and eventually find a stairway that goes up but not back into the church. I realize that I will be late for Mass so I look around for a way to get back into the church. I finally find a stairway that takes me outside, and I discover that there is more to the church out here too. I continue to walk around, but I don't find a door to take me back in.

I tell our writers how I interpret this dream for myself and how I think it reflects on us as a group. I find two levels of meaning in it for me at this time in my life. I am in the church, in an involved, intimate way. I am at home with walking through the sanctuary and being in the sacristy. But this day, I find that the CD I had placed there is gone. When I realize that I think I no longer have a voice in this church.

I intend to continue as a member and participate in the Eucharist, but the only stairway that I can find takes me to the underground church. There I find some darkness, but a sense of being at home. The towers I find there look like the outside walls of my childhood parish church—a grand Romanesque building where my faith was nurtured.

As I try to go back into the church, the only way that is open to me is from the outside. I am in the churchyard—another dark, mysterious, but comfortable space.

The second level of meaning my dream has for me is that I go from being in the church to being in the depths of my own soul where I find a fertile, fallow garden and my rootedness in faith. It is a rich and mysterious place of great depth and beauty where the treasures of my soul speak to me and invite me to feel at home.

This is my journey as a woman in today's church. I find my strength in my deep inner resources where a spirituality rooted in tradition is about to burst forth in fruitfulness and to flourish. It is not just my journey, but our journey together as we invite each other into our inner wells and gardens and caves and discover and share the riches we find there and gain strength from each other so that we find our voices and can speak these truths when we move out of the hidden inner spaces into the public sphere of church and community.

I find myself crying as I finish telling the group about my dream and its significance for me. Jane has been standing behind me, on the other side of the sofa where I am sitting. She places her left hand on my right shoulder and gives me an affectionate and consoling squeeze. There is silence.

Resurrection

Suzanne Falvey

Suzanne yearns for a contemplative, somewhat sedate life near her New England coastal roots. Instead, with her family she finds herself navigating life, rich with activity, in a large Midwestern town. To the amusement of family and friends, she claims her dog Dale gives her the balance she so desperately craves.

Here she writes about her oldest son whom she and her partner adopted fifteen years ago. He is developmentally disabled. When they got him Suzanne explained, "Cornell didn't speak. We got him a pet to help him express himself, at least emotionally. He noticed that the other children would call Lightening and he would run to them. So Cornell learned to speak so he could call his dog. Then, after he began to speak, he had profound things to share with the rest of us." Suzanne describes how she learned to appreciate her faith by seeing Cornell come alive when they went to church. The family changed from becoming an occasional church-going family to a regular church-attending one because of Cornell. His great and abiding faith brought all of them back to church. He is the boy. The boy who called her forth from his silence.

It was the boy understood by no one. The boy who spoke no words but typed "church is important." It was the boy who poured bran flakes in her shoes. The boy that threw her furniture. The boy that finally found the word "Bitch." It was the boy who hit, kicked, bit, and spat.

It was the boy. The boy with the saucer brown eyes and soft brown skin. The boy with no words. The boy locked within his own mind. The boy locked tight within the social service system. It was the boy that cried himself to sleep. It was the boy with sullen silence who brought her back.

It was the boy, all alone. The boy longing for safety. It was the boy kicked out of school. It was the boy with no friends. It was the boy looking at Chaucer, said not to read. The boy, laughing infectiously. The boy "obviously" not there. It was the boy with the charming wink. The boy with Houdini-like tricks, who brought her back over and over and over again, willing her to risk praying once more.

She always longed to belong. The altar dress she was told she could never wear. The bells that rang in mystery that she could not ring. Oh, she was allowed to read the words. Proclaimed them even, to communities. She gathered the fifth graders, convincing them

Christ was real. She was chastised once by the priest. Her students were kneeling on the table, laughing drunk with the Holy Spirit. She led retreats. She passed the sacrament. But only once did she get to ring the bells.

She remembers it clearly. She was still a kid who thought she was no longer a kid. After reading the word. After watching the bread and wine being dressed. After kneeling, kneeling and kneeling, hidden behind two tall men, the white almost-priest and the black money collector. The least important. The most important. He was allowed to seat the people, collect the money, and ring the bells, announcing the Christ allowed to come only through the Father.

She remembers it clearly. In the silence that the host was raised. The brown hardened hands, strong and worn from collecting corn in the fields, raking in hay, cleaning the muck from people's toilet lines. This man belonged to his hands, the only color in town besides the pompous dress in the pew. He laughs as they tell the story that she cried as a baby to shake his hand, thinking he was dirty.

She felt his gentle warm hand touch hers, raising it gently, quietly, defiantly. Together they set their eyes on the gold, the gold that held the blood and the body that begged them to do it. He set her hand on the bells, the handle sizzling in her fist. Keeping her head still she turned her eyes. He nodded without moving. She lifted the bells, shaking them, unsure…but it was then that Jesus was raised. They never spoke of it. He knew in that moment she tasted the truth.

After ringing the bells she spent her time in school volunteering. Serving the poor. Joining ministries. Studying the word. It was rich. She believed it fed her soul. She doubts that now. It was the moments outside the dogma that abated her hunger. The moments with the teenage mother with HIV and four children. The moments watching the Jewish professor's children, adopted from somewhere in Asia, giggle and cry. The moment a friend threatened with a gun to her head to end her own life. She found life building outhouses for those without plumbing and heard the bells ringing as she held a dying Mexican baby who needn't have died. In far-off lands the church spread its rich propaganda while its youngest, its poorest had not a vaccine. She popped in and out of churches and found she liked them best empty.

As she sampled her Christ she befriended a soul whose company she would keep for a lifetime. The church disagreed so together they took their two lives to a backyard in September with friends and no family and defied the church once again. A man of the cloth, betraying his order, bestowed upon them the most holy of un-holy unions. He too had tasted her Christ.

And so it began with an unlikely union, the stirring of the boy with the vulnerable, saucer brown eyes. They decided to host him and hold him inside. He would be birthed from their hearts. They welcomed him into their home. When she first met him, she knew it was Jesus tugging her soul. Together, she prayed. The boy ran away in the day. The boy cried at night aloft in his bed. She fell asleep in the chair while flashlights on end blazed a hole to the heavens. Dead batteries and frustration caused the holes in her walls.

The boy needed safety to express the depth and pain in his being. The boy needed rhythm and chanting to sit still. The boy needed God to support her. The boy needed strength of forever. One day, the bounced around, cast away, salvation army boy who would spin things and stare typed "church is important."

The boy didn't know what he was saying. The boy had no idea what he was asking. She was comfortable with her "Christ in the church" at a distance. She long ago stowed it away. The church didn't want her "as is." Pontifical Wisdom: her mother love was abusive. Her marriage a sin. The church she had loved was forgotten until the boy with the saucer brown eyes. Duty to him, they started attending, all three. She laughed as she reflected, "rag-tag trinity." He began to get quiet and settled. His hand on hers on the missal as her Christ rose again.

He was obsessed with the water. She loved him for it, until he played in the font, spraying water above from below. It had to happen. That boy. The boy asked to become part of the church through the sprinkle of water. The boy who bit others. The boy who made teachers cry. The boy who could charm his way out of trouble did not understand. His body, the government ruled. The division, the workers, the courts told him "no," stamping "denied" on his soul. The boy with no words. The boy with no voice simply typed. "I belong to no one. Not even God."

The unholy union. The abusive love. The sinful marriage. The rag-tag trinity all came together. Her Christ rising again. Of course the boy would be sprinkled. She knew too well the sorrow. The boy must belong. And so, defying papal suggestion, they became family, holy in name. The boy, now official, bathed in the spirit. The boy who could not pronounce words sang syllables loudly. The boy who could not control his hands received on his tongue. The boy, presenting his sins in exchange for redemption, years later confirmed in his call. He was only a boy.

The boy brought her back. The boy caused her tears. The boy made her laugh. The boy challenged her definitions. The boy reminded her she disliked being angry. The boy saw the pain in her soul. The boy forced her back to her Love. The boy led her into forgiveness. The boy swallowed the church and sweated out the love of her Christ. Over and over and over and over again, the boy made her stare at her crucifixion. Together. He witnessed her resurrection. It was the boy with the soft brown skin. The boy with the saucer brown eyes.

Hot Summer Day

Martha C. Rodriguez

Martha is a devoted mother, grandmother, and great grandmother who feels so blessed. On life's challenging, joyful, and purposeful journey, she strives to "have good heart" (Buddha), and to live a life of love and compassion with no hidden agenda. And while that may sound too ambitious, with inevitable struggle, Martha insists on trying. She believes that each relationship has, at its heart, a holy purpose.

It was a hot summer day, probably in July. Our family was in our 1936 black four-door Chevy, going west on the dusty Red Rock Road toward the little town of Gardner, Colorado. My father was driving, of course, and my mother and youngest sister Lucy were in the front seat. In the back seat I sat in the middle; my brother Joe sat on my left next to the window, and my sister Maggie sat on my right, also sitting next to the coveted window. The seating arrangement, as I look back, reflected my station in the family. I am a middle child, with a brother and a sister older, and a brother and a sister younger, although at this time, my youngest brother Rod had yet to be born. We were the children of Fred and Mary. The first four of us were born a year apart, and my youngest brother was eight years younger than me.

It was about eleven in the morning. Suddenly my father stopped the car at the side of the road, and my mother and I got out. It had already been determined that I would accompany my mom, and the rest of the kids would go with my dad.

My mother and I proceeded to walk down this obviously little-traveled, uneven, and at places, rocky mountainous road. I followed my mom, walking as fast as I could to keep up. The winds were strong. On three occasions my petite six-year-old body was unable to negotiate the rough road, the sudden gusts of wind, and my inexperience in mountainous country. Each time I fell, my mom stopped to look back and check if I was all right. Of course I was. I was a city girl, but a tough little tomboy, better at boy activities than boys my age and some even a little older. I'm sure I would have fallen more often were it not for my natural grasp of body movements that had not been limited by the social teachings of how a girl behaves. So I got up quickly and just went on. Any pain, scratches, or bruises sustained, I ignored, as I was probably not even aware of them.

We finally arrived at this little farmhouse that my mother grew up in and was now vacant—everyone had moved away in pursuit of a better life. We walked through the mostly empty house 'til we got to the room where the altar was. There were beautiful religious pictures, statues, candles, and other (I suspect personal) items that had been left behind.

My mother cleaned and dusted, lit some candles, knelt, and at times stood before the altar. She prayed the rosary, and from her prayer book. I sat in a chair quietly and watched her in total acceptance and love for her, always feeling secure in her love for me. Looking back, I am certain she was in a lot of pain, and yet, as throughout her life, she was steadfast in her faith in God, to whom she turned for solace and help. She lived a life of trust in God and acceptance of His will, and she is the one from whom I have learned that.

After a certain time we walked back to the place on the road where we had been dropped off. My father picked us up, and we drove the sixty miles back home. On the way home my parents discussed my father's visit to his family. For you see, my mother was fiercely at odds with his family and refused to mingle with them.

As I reflect on that day so long ago, I think about the ways in which I've become like my mother…how I've come to embody her traits—her deep faith and her fierceness—traits by which others see me as strong, willful, fair-minded, but sometimes forbidding. And I try to retread the path that brought me to this place…

As a child I struggled for a place among my siblings and peers, struggled for what I felt was my due. I was a tenacious and determined little person, especially if challenged. But according to family stories, my relatives seemed to find those qualities amusing, so they tolerated my scrappiness and my curiosity.

I was often left to my own devices growing up—an ignored middle child—though some would say that because I was self-sufficient, it was easier to let me ramble than to try to rein me in. I remember scurrying around a family farm with my cousins and scouring the neighborhood with my brother. We'd do mostly "boys' stuff," especially playing ball, which was my favorite thing in the world. And I was better at it than most of the boys. Then puberty set in.

My family, especially my older sister, would often call me stubborn. I remember one occasion when I was so angry with my sister that I surprised her from behind, wrapping my arms around her and knocking her down to the ground. Even though she was two years older, she wouldn't fight me. She went into the house, with both elbows bloodied, and told our mother. I can still see her slender body in a green and black print dress, crying and walking back into the house. I regretted my actions almost immediately, and even now when I think of her, I feel ashamed.

My mother's reprimand was uncharacteristically mild that day; at other times her punishment—usually verbal—could be crushing. I don't believe she realized the damage she inflicted, not having had the benefit of an education past the third grade. My father was a good provider, and I never went hungry, but he was emotionally absent to me. I don't recall ever having had anyone with whom to share my thoughts, so although I felt safe, my loneliness must have been pervasive.

Despite the lack of expressed affection, I felt then—and I now know—that my mother loved me deeply. Rarely did I doubt it. She modeled a reliance on her powerful faith as a source of strength during trials and tribulations. With the aid of prayer and hard work, she struggled to do the right thing—and always with integrity. Her faith, fierceness, and sense of integrity allowed her to bear sadness, fears, and betrayals.

I appreciate my mother's determination to give us a Catholic education. I graduated from high school with strong academic skills, and I launched myself into the world not realizing how important that education would become.

Within six months after graduation, I married and was on my way to Germany where I gave birth to a beautiful son born during the thalidomide scourge. Although he was born with a deformed right hand, we felt fortunate that his infirmity was minor, compared to the thousands of other children who were born with severe deformities. I subsequently gave birth to two beautiful daughters and—for the sake of us all—divorced their alcoholic father, returned to my home town, got a job, searched for grants, received two, and got a degree in nursing. In between, I remarried, and then divorced in 1977. In 1984 my fine, responsible son was murdered at the age of twenty-six. Dazed by that experience, I found both distraction and purpose by returning to school, and in 1989 I graduated with a master's degree in guidance and counseling.

My daughters faltered, but with their strong sense of right as a compass, they've re-gained their footing, and today I feel blessed with two wonderful, sensitive, self-respecting, hard-working and responsible women who have been a great source of pride and comfort.

My youngest bravely declared her lesbian orientation at the age of twenty-two. I was not surprised, as I had already sensed that truth about her…and not only because I am her mother, but also because I am a lesbian. I had put off declaring it, because in my town my children would have been exposed to public rancor, and I didn't want to subject my extended family to the embarrassment I know they would have felt. I openly declared my lesbianism to my daughters after I retired and moved closer to where they both lived. They were not surprised either. I am now open to my immediate family and relatives. It seems not to have mattered to any of us, as I feel we have inherited my mother's power of faith, fine tuned her ferocity, and imitated her unquestionable love. I can still hear her sigh after a valiant fight, whether successful or not, "a la mano de Dios," and after a good day, "Thanks to my God."

I have survived, thrived—and thanks to my God—I am still actively striving at age seventy-five toward ensuring that I fulfill my life's purpose.

Where I First Met God

Lacey Louwagie

Lacey Louwagie lives in South Dakota, where she shares a tiny house with her husband, one dog, two cats, two fish, and hundreds of books. She loves being snowed in, writing speculative fiction, and pondering God. She is co-editor of Hungering and Thirsting for Justice *(ACTA Publications, 2012), a collection of true stories by young adult Catholics.*

When I was a small child, I thought the priest at our local parish was God. (Little did I know the Catholic Church would later try to sell me on a very similar idea: that the priest was somehow a more valid "stand-in" for Jesus than anyone else—especially a woman. By that time, I wasn't buying it.) Perhaps I came to believe the priest was God because when I whined about going to church, Mom always said that God gave us so much; the least we could do was see Him once a week. The priest was ancient—as surely God must be!—and despite the way he stooped when he walked and mumbled when he talked, he had a kindly face and disposition. When I look back, I feel amazed that I could believe that was *really* God standing at the altar and yet still find the service a bore!

Although both my parents were raised Catholic, my mom was the only one in her family who continued to practice as an adult. The Catholic Church was something of a novelty to my cousins on my mom's side. Once, taking a walk with an older cousin, we stopped at the Catholic church in her town. The doors were open, so we went inside. I marveled at the statues, the balcony, the paintings, and the beauty that was both familiar and new at the same time. We both knelt for some perfunctory prayers. I pointed toward the altar and said, "That's where God stands."

She raised an eyebrow. "You mean, the priest?"

"No, I mean God."

She gestured at the altar. "The *priest* stands up there."

"In *our* church, it's God."

She chuckled. "I'm pretty sure it's the priest."

I was embarrassed that my older, cooler cousin found this amusing. I never mistook the priest for God again—much to the annoyance of many in the Catholic hierarchy, I'm sure!

By the time I was ten, my parish had probably voted me "least likely to remain Catholic." I was a thorn in my teachers' sides, constantly demanding better reasons why women couldn't be ordained and editing my workbooks to use gender-inclusive language. I read the edited version when it was my turn to read aloud. After one class in which I'd changed about a million "he's" to "s/he's," a friend and partner in dissent declared with me that, as soon as we were adults, we were going to be "anything but Catholic."

But by the time I was thirteen, the Catholic Church had become the most stable force in my life. My dad had gone back to school, and my mom had started working outside the home for the first time. I was suffering bullying at school and caring for my younger sister at home. Perhaps the worst changes of all were those happening within my own body. Desperate to return to the comparative purity and simplicity of childhood, I sought that purity and simplicity in the church. The church provided a structure lacking everywhere else and offered a false sense of control. I began bargaining with God, and Catholicism provided so many bargaining tools! *I'll pray a whole rosary every night if You let me not get my period during school; I'll prostrate myself and pray from now until I hear the car in the driveway, if You'll make sure my parents get home safely; I will obey the rules of the church, I won't complain about going to Mass, I will stop resenting and questioning and making fun of the priest when he sings if You can make my life make sense again.*

It wasn't all about bargaining though. I started to feel the real spiritual comfort of Catholicism—the tangibility of my grandmother's red rosary beads slipping through my fingers, the stiffness in my knees after kneeling through the Eucharistic prayer, the Host gently dissolving on my tongue, the predictable rhythm of the Litany of Saints—and of course, Mary. Catholicism gave me Mary when I was angry with a male God; it was Mary I prayed to when my menstrual cramps doubled me over with pain or when the sticky blood between my legs just wouldn't stop coming. My prayer was simple: "Mary, help me. *You* understand."

Perhaps it was because of Catholicism that my developing sexuality was a barely realized whisper in my adolescence. What had been a childhood fascination with sex quickly turned into a shameful secret under my religious education teachers' instruction. Sex was so fraught with guilt and distress that I gladly embraced the church's teaching about abstinence—best not to have to deal with it at all! Although my sexual education had included a definition of the word "gay," I understood implicitly that there were no gay people where I lived. Gay was something that happened far away.

And so, because every person in my whole world expected that I would grow to love boys and men, I expected it, too. Meeting those expectations came naturally enough; my first crushes were on male teachers, and then on boys in my class. I wasn't consciously aware of any same-sex attraction except that I ached under the homophobic social norms that made it taboo to touch my best friend. We rode the same bus, and after she got off, I often spent the remainder of the ride trying not to think about how nice it would be if she could just put her head on my shoulder. Thoughts like this raised a panic within me: *Ohmygod does this mean I'm gay?* I dealt with this terrifying question in two ways. First, I replaced the image of my best friend in my mind with whoever was the least onerous boy in my class. See, that would feel nice, too, right? *Right.* Good. Not gay. Second, I'd imagine having sex with a woman—because being gay was really about wanting to have sex with women, right? The thought of having sex with a woman didn't appeal to me. I never considered the fact that having sex with *anyone* at age thirteen wasn't appealing. All I knew was that the crisis was averted. I loved my best friend, but I wasn't gay.

The deal should have been sealed when I was sixteen and fell in love with Drew, a man I cantored with at church. My love for Drew was wrapped up in my love for Catholicism, until I couldn't really separate the two. I loved going to church because it meant I would stand beside him for an hour and that he would take my hand during the "Our Father" and smile at me first during the sign of peace. The smell of the paper in the missalettes was the scent of Drew; the Eucharistic host dissolving on my tongue was the hope for his kiss. Love letters to God and to Drew filled my journal. I asked God whether I was using Catholicism to get close to Drew, or whether God was using Drew to bring me closer to Him.

But then I had the dream: I was "messing around" with another woman. She had dark black curls and glowing tan skin; I knew nothing about her except that she was beautiful, and that I wanted her. I awoke terrified. This was it, I thought. I really was gay, and my life was over. I had left high school early to start college, so I was at least outside the environment that had taught me that being gay might be the very worst thing I could be. Even so, I pushed the possibility away as hard as I could. I looked away from the posters around campus during gay pride week, left the living room when TV news reported on teachers being fired for being gay, skimmed but never, *ever* read articles about Ellen DeGeneres coming out. Despite my best efforts, the reality that homosexuality existed confronted me everywhere I went. I wished I could pretend that it didn't exist; if it didn't exist, then it couldn't be happening to me.

I was still in love with Drew, but somehow I thought a single homoerotic desire had the power to eradicate every attraction I'd ever felt for males. When I watched movies, I would obsess over the female and male leads—which one did I *really* think was more attractive? I did the same with the men and women in my poetry class. There was a boy who sat in front of me with curly blond hair, wire-frame glasses, broad shoulders, and an intellectual air. I found him attractive, didn't I? Phew, I must be straight. But that boy didn't make the girl in the same class go away—the one with the red hair so vibrant that it was almost maroon, the one who wore bright yellow tights under her shorts and wrote poems comparing seedless watermelon to abortion. *She* was the one I'd noticed on the first day of class.

Finally, I confronted the reality that somehow, both of these attractions *did* exist within me. I *was* truly attracted to men . . . and to women. I sat alone in the stairwell outside my bedroom, my head held in my hands, when the thought entered my consciousness for the first time: maybe I was bisexual. As soon as I'd named it, a homophobic solution came on its heels: I would just decide not to pursue my attraction to women. Ironically, this is pretty much exactly what the Catholic Church tells me to do.

But neither Catholicism nor Christianity figured into my fear of being gay. I certainly didn't fear what God would think. No, my fear came from knowing I'd have to keep this secret or risk being ostracized by my community. I knew what the Catholic Church's stance was; long before I thought it applied to me, I looked up homosexuality in the catechism, and I'd heard plenty of Christian preachers blast their opinions about it. But none of it took root. Even when I was most susceptible to the clear-cut answers mainstream Christianity and Catholicism provided—especially regarding sex—they never had any authority with me when it came to homosexuality. I think of St. Augustine's reference to "the law that is written in ~~men's~~ [all] hearts and cannot be erased no matter how sinful they are." The law God wrote on my heart was one of love and acceptance. And I simply knew that, on this matter, mainstream Christianity was wrong.

I thought I'd arrived at a prudent solution: I could inwardly acknowledge who I really was while also pursuing only love that I could declare publicly, only love that didn't entail the risk of being cast out of my community. But the solution must not have been too great after all, because I fell into the worst depression of my life.

God blessed me with chronic migraines. It didn't *feel* like a blessing when I spent most of my teenage years curled up on the couch, my eyes closed against the pain, holding perfectly still to keep from vomiting. But in a rural community where people are still expected to "pull themselves up by their bootstraps" when they're struggling with mental illness, those migraines were my ticket to help. After a long summer of unsuccessful medications, I got a prescription for the antidepressant Elavil. It cut my migraines down from one a day to one or two a month. More important, it saved me from my depression.

Without the depression's fog over my life, I didn't worry about sexual orientation throughout the remainder of college. I read books with lesbian main characters without feeling afraid to identify with them. I considered myself "about 85% straight," but I had accepted that sexuality existed on a continuum. I didn't dwell on occasional attractions toward other women. I kept in touch with Drew and had a brief Internet romance with another man, but otherwise made it through college free of romantic entanglements. My most compelling relationships were the ones I had with my female friends.

After college, I moved to Duluth for an internship. I loved the city but didn't know a single soul within it. That's when I started realizing how much other people's expectations and assumptions affected my self-perception. When there were no family members or friends reflecting back their understanding of "who Lacey is," I began to feel set adrift, anchored by nothing, perhaps at risk of fading away entirely. It was terrifying.

After nearly a year there, I started taking guitar lessons from Jenny, a woman who was a few years older than me. I still hadn't formed emotional attachments to anyone nearby, and I thought I would lose it if I saw one more warm smile or embrace that wasn't for me. But because of the lessons, being alone wasn't such a heavy burden anymore; it gave me the opportunity to practice and experiment—an experimentation that soon went beyond my music. I listened to tapes of our lessons when I practiced and when I fell asleep at night. I started attending Jenny's gigs, and I couldn't take my eyes off her. Butterflies gathered in my stomach whenever I stood outside her door, waiting for the student before me to finish. One night, driving home from one of her performances, the realization of what it all meant flooded over me: I had a crush on Jenny. And I wasn't afraid. I was elated. She was in a relationship with a man, and I knew nothing would come of my attraction. But it felt *so good* to step into my whole self at last.

After that night, at the age of twenty-two I started openly identifying as bisexual. I caught up on my gay reading and film, sported rainbows, and became an activist for equality. Later that year, when I met Jayme's ocean-blue eyes for the first time at a party, I knew exactly what it meant. I was totally ready. If I had loved Drew because of Catholicism, I loved Jayme because she was everything else. She was Tibetan prayer flags, karma, and hands dirty from gardening; she was walking barefooted through autumn leaves and the taste of rose petals. I fell harder than I'd ever fallen for anyone. I wrote her love letters, too—but this time, I sent them. Thoughts about how my family, hometown, or the rest of society would react were barely a blip on my radar. The culture's scorn would be a small price to pay for the chance to be with Jayme.

But even as I'd finally come home to my sexuality, I hadn't found a spiritual home after more than a year of "church shopping." When I first moved, I'd visited churches and denominations that were more liberal than Catholicism, knowing that my values were out of line with many "official" church teachings. But even churches where I was aligned with the values didn't feel like home. I missed the Crucifix and the Eucharist. Although the other churches had depictions of Jesus on the altar, it was hard for me to find Him anyplace other than in one unwelcoming, conservative Catholic parish after another. Finally, while attending a work retreat on the far side of town, I got lost and ended up outside the only local Catholic church I'd never attended. Wondering whether there was even a point to it anymore, I checked it out the following weekend. When the priest gave a homily about his own struggle with depression and the social stigma surrounding it, I knew I'd found my church home at last.

And although Jayme and I didn't work out as a couple, we retained a deep friendship that continues to enrich my life. Last year, I brought her to church with me. It felt good to have these two parts of my life converge at last. As I drove us home, she said, "The service was nice." Then she paused, and continued, "But doesn't it bother you that you have to say you aren't worthy?"

Lord, I am not worthy to receive You, but only say the word and I shall be healed.

I said quickly, "Well, it's about humility." But after my initial defensive reaction, I let her question sink in. I admitted, "Yeah, I guess it sort of does bother me."

For how many times had the feeling of being unworthy weighed upon my shoulders? It began with sermons about why women couldn't be priests and continued with the church's resistance to gender-inclusive language. It was in the official church doctrine that called homosexual acts "intrinsically disordered," with no acknowledgment of the deep love that could be manifested in those acts. It was in the papal decree that men who had "homosexual tendencies" should not enter the priesthood and should be weeded out when suspected—side by side with prayers about the priest shortage! It was in pamphlets scattered at Catholic events about "what the church says about same-sex marriage," and petitions at the entrance of the church in support of the "Defense of Marriage Act." It was in the way my feet dragged as I climbed the church steps, wondering why I still did this

Sunday after Sunday. I understood the message coming from the hierarchy: they didn't really want an unrepentant feminist and openly bisexual woman in their midst. A priest once told me that, "It would be better if everyone who doesn't agree with all the church's teachings would leave. It would result in a smaller church, but a purer one."

I wonder what Jesus would say about this "purer" church. I remember that Jesus, too, worked within a failing system for social justice. Despite the priests who had tried to convince me that women couldn't be priests *because Jesus was a man,* I'd begun to notice something they never mentioned. Jesus's body might have been a man's, but the example he set was a woman's. Like a woman, he gathered children on His lap when no one else had time for them, and like a woman He refused to respond to violence with violence. Like a woman, His life was one of thankless service to others. Jesus was a paradigm of androgyny who, like me, loved without distinction for sex or gender.

So I continue to climb those steps every Sunday, because I know I am not alone in my struggle for a more just church. Being Catholic is so much a part of my life and my history that I've accepted that it's unchangeable—just like being bisexual is unchangeable. I love both parts of me. And the more I love and accept the person God created me to be, the more I love all of God's people and the more I love God. I know now that the priest at the altar isn't God, but the Catholic Church was where I first met God, nonetheless. And that is not something from which I can turn easily away.

This essay was originally published in the anthology *Unruly Catholic Women Writers: Creative Responses to Catholicism*, Jeana DelRosso, Leigh Eicke, and Ana Kothe, (Eds.), copyright © 2013, State University of New York Press, Albany, NY.

In Thankfulness to God and Marianne

Shawn Kelly

Shawn is a spirit-filled singer/songwriter who enjoys spending time with her partner of twenty years and their two rescued dogs, Rennie and Wall-E. She enjoys outdoor adventures and once journeyed to the base camp of Mount Everest. Though multiple sclerosis has now limited her abilities, it hasn't limited her hope. Shawn weekly spreads that hope—and her smile—at a men's shelter in Philly, and she truly believes she receives more than she gives.

Twenty years ago, God placed a wonderful woman in my life—one who would share my struggles, triumphs, and most importantly, my love of Him.

For as long as I can remember, I have been a spiritual, thankful person. But it wasn't until God put adversity in my life that I realized just how much more thankful and spiritual I could be—and how much deeper my relationship with Him *would* be, as a result. People wonder how I can be so thankful for this adversity, but I've learned, as I view the many struggles of the world and see my own friends and neighbors carrying far greater burdens than I, that things can be a whole lot worse. Through it all, God has been there. And when Marianne came into my life twenty years ago, God was there, too. I believe God *put* her there.

Five years ago, I lost my thirty-nine-year-old sister, the result of a ventricular arrhythmia—one that left her in a coma for two weeks, with Marianne and me spending almost every night in the hospital with her, hoping and praying she would wake up. She never did. Of course I did the usual thing, asking "Why, God?" But through this awful tragedy—one that left three boys without a mother and me without a sister—I know that God never left us. Not my parents, not her husband, not her children, not me. And Marianne never left us, either.

About ten months after my sister's death, I made the trip to Richmond, Virginia, to tell my grieving parents that I had just been diagnosed with multiple sclerosis (MS). God was there, giving me the strength and courage to share with my parents my own hope that things would be okay. Marianne was there, too, and today she is my rock on Earth. And He is the foundation upon which everything has been built in my life. Among His many lessons to me in the course of this disease is this: that the *only* thing within my control is my attitude about what is happening to me. I have absolutely no control over anything else, and I am at peace with that because I have come to trust God fully after the work I've seen him perform in my life.

He's working in the lives of my family, too. For years, my brother has struggled with bipolar disorder, suffering from suicidal thoughts that have resulted in his hospitalization more than once. In his worst state, he lost the ability to work and spent hours holed up in his apartment with no sense of self-worth. Seeing his pain, Marianne spoke to him, wrote to him, and was there for him, as she was for me when I began to feel helpless. I speak in the past tense not because he's no longer with us, and not because one is ever *healed* from this awful prison, but because God was there and has allowed my brother to find his self-worth again. God gave my brother a great ability to connect with people. He found him a community organization that offered services to the mentally ill and, later, gave him the courage to volunteer there. Afterward, with God's help, my brother enrolled in a five-month program where he trained to become a certified peer-counselor and even graduated at the top of his class. I know that God is working in *his* life, and because I love my brother, I know He's working in mine. I feel *convinced* of God's presence now, and I've come to realize that He was also with me thirteen years ago when I was facing the darkest time of my life.

That was when God gave me the courage to own my true identity—to tell my family about Marianne. I was scared to death. It was the hardest thing I'd ever faced. I was the child who had *never* given my parents any trouble. I was the model youth group member, member of the church choir, the perfect Catholic. Catholics aren't okay with homosexuals—well, maybe if they're chaste and suffering, they are. At least, that's what I was told. But I'd also learned that lying was a sin, too, and I could no longer bear the weight of lying in order to hide my true self.

I told my parents and siblings in a letter, which is something I regret. I just knew that if I had tried to speak directly to my parents without a carefully thought-out letter, I could never explain things adequately. The problem was, I wasn't there to accompany the letter. And because it caused my parents so much pain, it's something I wish I could change to this day. So what followed were a few awkward and painful phone calls and questions from them, my responses to which could not calm their fears. Then, a year of nothing—not even a birthday call. Darkness, yet hope.

The weight had been lifted. I was free. They say that time is the great healer, and they're right. After a year, my parents and I found our way back to each other, and over the years, they've seen Marianne steadfast in her position by my side and the family's, even through our adversity. They truly love her.

God is so good. He placed a wonderful woman in my life. And together, we would thank God that He gave us the courage to be ourselves in our church. When we became members of our past two parishes, we met with the pastors to introduce ourselves as a *couple,* making sure that we were welcome *together.* No, we held no expectations that the priests would stand on the altar and say, "Let's welcome the new homosexual couple to our church." We simply needed to know, before we gave our time, talent, and treasure, that we were welcome there, as we *are.*

Today, we are active members who participate in a monthly faith-sharing group, where each member shares how the upcoming week's Gospel reading speaks to us—not in a bible study sort of way, but in a *personal* way. Early on in the group, we were sharing our thoughts about one of the many readings that deal with judgment. I felt God calling me to open up about my true self, in order to have a more meaningful discussion about what judgment means to me. Once again He was asking me to have faith in Him, because He knew that He had put me in open, loving arms with this group of people. And He had done just that. Today, we continue— all of us—to explore more deeply through faith. God is truly good.

We've also witnessed the love of Catholic parents who, several years ago, started a ministry for gay and lesbian Catholics because they *knew* there were lost gay and lesbian Catholics who needed support. They were right. And Marianne and I are deeply grateful to them for their courage to start this group and for the unconditional love they show us. In fact, so many of the people whom we've met through our church are a blessing to us. But it is because God gave us the courage to be our true selves that we met them. *They* are among the many reasons we continue to have faith in the Catholic Church so that, one day, our homosexual children will no longer have to hide. I know that God is faithful to those who trust in Him, and He has truly been faithful to me, bringing me through hardships and bringing love into my life. Wow, God is so good.

Life at 808

Grace Conroy, OP

Grace Conroy has been a Dominican living on the West Coast for more than 50 years and a pilgrim on the journey of life, finding God in the most unlikely places! She is energized by oceans and rivers, movies and live theater. Her mantra is: The Spirit of the Lord is upon me and has anointed me to bring the Gospel to any and all who need/desire to hear the Good News!

"Hearing to speech is never one-sided. Once a person is heard to speech, she becomes a hearing person." (Nelle Morton, *The Journey Is Home*)

When I was about twelve I announced to the family, "When I grow up I am going to write a book." My aunt asked what I would title the book. "Life at 808," I proclaimed as if it were an accomplished fact. The family nodded and thought that was a good title; they weren't so sure about the content. Life was always a little wonderful and wacky at 808. Friends and family would come and go and there was always a lot of laughter and "a raising of the glasses."

A great old building—that was 808. One of the charms was a winding stairway leading to the roof that offered a huge panoramic view of the city—a girl could dream many dreams up there and assume roles that "might happen." At that time, being lesbian was nowhere on my radar screen!

We are a small family, so "family" included, and still includes, many persons outside the conventional definition, i.e., a mother, a father, and offspring. We were an extended family long before that term became popular, and our family experience was my *first awakening* that there was more than one way to do or become something. One could still be family and yet not connected by blood or marriage.

Despite our different family configuration, my childhood was rather ordinary. I had a traditional Catholic school education, beginning in kindergarten. One side of my family was Catholic, the other Protestant. My *second awakening* was when Sister prepared us for our First Communion. One of the things we learned was that "only baptized Catholics would go to heaven." I was only seven years old, but my mind would not go there. My father was not baptized, but he was a good man. So I knew that the church was wrong about that, even if I couldn't articulate it.

Those memories date from the early to mid 1950s, a time when life seemed more predictable, and roles were clearly defined (or at least we thought they were). Everyone knew what was right and wrong, mortal and venial sins were impressed on children at an early age, and confessionals on Saturday afternoon had long lines. Lesbians and gays were closeted, and the terms were never uttered on anyone's lips, at least not in my family.

In 1956 I entered a teaching congregation on the West Coast. At sixteen my reasons for entering seemed clear: to serve God and to teach. Now I understand that "our call" has many threads, like the warp and woof of a fabric, and that vocation is part of God's mysterious plan for each of us.

When I made my first profession in 1959, our vow ceremonies were focused on giving up worldly ideas and pleasures. This focus flowed from a spirituality that placed the emphasis on a personal relationship with Jesus, which was to be contained in a life lived between the convent and the school.

However, the Spirit was quietly blowing and would soon bring an earthshaking change. There would be a rebirth in the church that had remained the same for centuries. On January 25, 1959, the same year I made my first profession, Pope John XXIII made the announcement that he was convening a Second Vatican Council. Little did we know what was to happen as a result of that council. One of the major documents, *Perfectae Caritatis*, urged religious communities to renew and return to the roots of their foundresses.

Not all communities renewed in the same way or at the same time. My community chose to enter renewal early on, and we not only "widened our tents," but we removed "the flaps" and took a new view of what was in our midst. We realized that the relationship to which Jesus called us went far beyond our narrowly construed worldview. This was the beginning of the unraveling of centuries' old traditions about religious life. Not too many years later, we had the option of returning to our baptismal names, habits became optional, and ministries were no longer assigned but discerned between the sister and her major superior.

We read and studied *Lumen Gentium* and rediscovered that we all are called, through our baptismal promises, to share in the common priesthood of Jesus. My *third awakening* was that we all have a vocation—some to marriage, some to religious life, some to the single life, and yes, some to ordained priesthood. The lifestyles are different, but they are not ordered in a hierarchical pattern making one better than the other. We also realized that the church was the people of God, the community. Church was not just the institution.

The theologian Walter Brueggemann describes a prophet as one who speaks the truth, even if it is unpopular and people don't want to hear it. As we entered renewal more deeply, we discovered that we were called to be prophets and to bring the Good News to the broken-hearted, the poor, and the vulnerable. We understood that one of our roles as religious women was to stand on the edges, which although it is not safer, does provide a broader perspective. What is this Good News we are called to preach today? Simply put, it is:

That all persons are deserving of respect and dignity

That all are welcomed at the Table

That we are all called to preserve life—life of the unborn; of the elderly; of the criminals; of those whose race, color, creed or sexual orientation is different from our own; of the creators of war who cause innocent lives to end prematurely.

Not everyone is comfortable or interprets the Good News according to these principles. For me, it has impacted and stretched how I define and live out my spirituality. Today I would describe spirituality as a movement of the Spirit that influences how I live out my relationship with God and others and manifests itself in the values and actions of my life.

During my first few years of teaching, there were moments when I would question whether or not I had made the right decision. The dangers of "particular friendships" were well known and navigating that landscape was tricky, but at this stage in my life, it was not an issue. I suspected that I felt differently from most of the sisters I knew. I felt out of step, but there was really no one with whom I could talk about it. These were the early 1960s, and in those days sexual orientation was not discussed. Unfortunately in most religious communities, sexuality itself was rarely mentioned! Because I did not feel any attraction to men or develop "crushes" on the parish priest or male teachers, I thought celibacy was a breeze.

Nineteen sixty-nine, the year of the Stonewall Riots, was a crucial time for me. Many of my companions in religious life were leaving. Although there were numerous reasons, many felt the call to marry and bear children. The women's movement was re-awakening, and suddenly we questioned why we were considered "lesser or inferior" to men. The civil rights movement had begun only a few years before, and our culture struggled with integration and equality. Liberation theology was just coming out of Latin America. For many it was a time to question whether or not this was where God wanted us. My *awakening* at this time led me to feel that this was where God wanted me and where I wanted to be. I was living my vocation, my call. My ministry was fruitful and fulfilling. I was living out the principles of Vatican II, and I loved my work with students and their parents. About ten years later, I was called to congregational leadership. Although there were challenges and painful moments, it was a rewarding time.

By the eighties I had completed graduate studies in counseling and education, and the term *homosexuality* was beginning to appear in counseling and psychology textbooks. I was fortunate to have excellent professors who did not gloss over sexuality. For me, it was the *dawning and awakening* of a new understanding of who I was.

I not only had factual information about homosexuality, but I began making friends with men and women who were gay and lesbian. Little by little I started to realize that I had more in common with these new friends than with men and women who identified as heterosexual or straight. And I felt comfortable with that.

My watershed year came in the early nineties when I was volunteering at an International Parents, Families, and Friends of Lesbians and Gays (PFLAG) Conference. I heard a prominent lesbian writer tell her story. By the end of her story, I said to the stranger next to me, "I am a lesbian!" He just looked at me, patted my arm, and said "Congratulations." This has been *my most profound awakening*. According to Genesis, "Everything God created is good." I firmly believed that at age seven, and I still believe it.

For me, it means that I can celebrate who I am with a sense of rightness; my named identity now fits! I can speak my whole truth and not have to compartmentalize it or juggle agendas when working with other individuals or groups. My spirituality is through the lens of a woman who identifies as lesbian who is a vowed religious. This is what provides me with life-giving energy and motivation. It is the relationship I have between my God and me. But far from journey's end, this has been just the beginning. My past awakenings had nurtured me and brought me to this point where I chose to come out to my family, friends, and community all at once. It has been a decision that I have never regretted, and I have felt truly supported in this decision.

I have never believed that sexual orientation is a choice. I believe it is God-given and God's gifts are to be embraced, celebrated, and used to help build the reign of God—not to be hidden away in fear or shame.

"Coming out" is a process that happens gradually and in stages: a lot of self-reflection; slow and often painful sharing with one or two trusted individual friends; lots of tears and laughter; and then, as the identity becomes more secure and feels right, widening the circle of sharing the truth of who one is. As a celibate woman this unraveling has had its own twists and turns, but the final "naming, claiming, and celebrating" is a similar process for all of us who identify as lesbian.

Although there is more acceptance today for gays, lesbians, bisexuals, transgendered, queer, and identifying (GLBTQI) persons, there is still much fear and hate directed to this group and any group who is different. Fear fuels hatred and individuals become scapegoats. In 1998 Matthew Shepard was beaten and left to die on a fence in rural Wyoming. In 2003 Gwen (Eddie) Arajuo was killed because she was a transgendered teen, and in 2008 an elementary school boy, Lawrence King, was murdered because he acted gay. The fundamentalist and evangelical churches are strengthening their positions against homosexuals. For those of us who profess to be disciples of Jesus Christ how can we let this continue to happen?

Inclusive language is a sensitive issue for many women and men. I use it, where appropriate, in speaking and in writing. In my personal prayer life I find that, by switching genders for God and using feminine attributes, my prayer takes on a more real and deeply felt nature. For years I have suffered with the use of "him" and "he" and felt absolutely nothing in my relationship with God. But now it is rich and meaningful for me. This is one way in which I continue to nurture my relationship with God. Also, Sophia Wisdom is a frequent companion in my spiritual life.

When I was "newly out" and volunteering in the GLBTQI community, I was given an award for working with members of that community in the area of spirituality. Two of those present said to me that they were both amazed and proud that a "nun would get such an award" and "that someone representing the Catholic Church" would care enough to reach out to them. About the same time I was talking with a woman in my parish. The homilist had mentioned sexual orientation, and she was concerned. She shared with me that she didn't want to have the negative feelings shared by many preachers and people in the pew, but she didn't know anyone who was gay or lesbian. Had she known a gay or lesbian person, she believed she would feel differently. I just smiled and said, "I think you do know some but just don't know it!" These were occasions that fostered my decision to be "fully out to everyone." We all need role models, and LGBTQI youth and adults who are struggling with their sexuality and orientation need to see men and women who celebrate who they are, living their baptismal call faithfully, and challenging the stereotypes and assumptions that exist.

My faith in God/Shekinah/Mystery is strong, alive, and dynamic. My faith in the institution we call church is no longer the faith of a seven-year-old who didn't believe her father would go to hell because he wasn't baptized. It is a mature adult faith, borne out of study and prayer, conversation and *communio*—out of challenge and *disputatio*. It is a faith developed from reading Scripture and the signs of the times. In the words of an African proverb, we are called "to create the path by walking." We create that path by telling our stories and sharing our visions, by believing in a loving, compassionate, and faithful God whose grace empowers each of us "to hear another into speech."

I love my Catholic faith, the sense of ritual and community. It is a vital part of who I am and where my roots lie. I love breaking open the word and celebrating Eucharist. But I cringe when I hear words like "disordered human being, an abomination"; we can't let "those" people destroy marriage; the Bible says it is a sin; or we can accept the orientation, but not the activity. I cringe because these are words used against good and loving people. I cringe because these are words used against me. There are many denominations and faith traditions that use rhetoric virulently and fan the hate, but it doesn't make a difference. Catholicism is about universality, and that means everyone should be welcome at the table. I have been asked, in not the nicest way, why I stay. I stay because this is my church; it nurtures my faith and my relationship with the One who is Mystery. I want to stay and dissent, faithfully, from those whose thinking and speaking oppress and further marginalize people.

My faith and spirituality continue to be nurtured and to grow more deeply in a variety of ways. Worship takes different forms, such as occasionally sharing Eucharist with communities in open and affirming churches. My companions on the journey keep me faithful and honest; my companions challenge me when I don't speak the "truth with love" (St. Catherine of Siena). They sustain me as I live my journey.

I began this reflection by recalling my desire to write a book and title it *Life at 808*. This was not exactly the book I had in mind when I was twelve! However, I believe the title still has merit. It is my wonderful and whacky extended family that nurtured me, supported me, and felt that my telling them I was a lesbian was just one more chapter in the book! My series of *awakenings* are the road signs that I have discovered in my life journey.

Several years ago, I wrote a poem that describes my faith journey. It is titled "The Road":

> The road to Emmaus was just a road—a dusty ordinary road about seven kilometers long. And NOW, a road steeped in hope and promise—conversion, healing, peace, and understanding. And they knew Him in the breaking of the Bread.
>
> The road to Emmaus is an invitation and a call to turn our hearts around—to proclaim the Risen Christ—to heal the broken-hearted—to *be hope* to one another. And we knew Him in the breaking of the bread.
>
> Our Emmaus road is not unlike that of the disciples—along the road our eyes are opened:
>
> > To children, men, and women who suffer abuse at the hands of their "loved ones";
> >
> > To farm workers and others forced to work for low pay and unsafe conditions;
> >
> > To patriarchal laws that refuse to acknowledge the cries for an inclusive church and society;
> >
> > To those who suffer from racism, sexism, and homophobia and, as a result, live their lives less fully than they were meant to be;
> >
> > And we knew them in the breaking of the bread.
>
> The road to Emmaus is an ordinary road made extraordinary by open hearts, open eyes, and open ears. We are travelers along the road. We are witnesses of the Resurrection, called not merely to see but also to act; not merely to speak hope but to BE HOPE. And we knew one another in the breaking of the bread.

Reflections…

Love and Acceptance

I attended a diversity training program. I was on the volunteer staff for Anytown, a youth project for the National Conference for Community and Justice. We met at Washington University in St. Louis, a campus with massive stone buildings that give the impression of medieval European castles. We met in the George Warren Brown School of Social Work building, Brown Hall, in the third-floor conference room, a room with old-world elegance. There were seventy-two of us seated in a spiral. Though most of us sat with our backs to one another, I sat in the inner circle, where I could see the faces of the people across from me five rows deep. There was no agenda. The training consisted of a workshop in which process was the agenda. We waited until an issue was raised, and then we responded to it. Keisha began the conversation by saying, "I think what all of us are looking for is acceptance. Whenever I walk into a room, that is what is on my mind. Am I going to feel accepted in this group?" She sat down. Silence. It seemed an eternity before someone else spoke. I don't remember what the next person said or exactly how the conversation turned from there. I sat stunned by the simplicity and truthfulness of Keisha's statement. It is something I have thought about a lot since then.

Acceptance. It is key. Our women respond to it in different ways. We see how painful an initial rejection by her parents is for Shawn. We read Martha's story of family conflict and a little girl who faces it with innocence and strength. We note how Grace's early experience of an extended, inclusive family helped plant the seed of acceptance in her.

For me, as a white woman who lives in mainstream circles, acceptance is not something I have to think about very much. I walk into a room and see other people who look like me. I don't have to look around, feel out of place, or wonder if I will be accepted. It takes interacting with people who live on the edges, who experience life from the point of view of the minority, for me to be conscious of this. Yet it is also with me all the time. I just don't think about it because most of the people in my life look like me. But to understand how it is to be different, I have put myself in places where I am different, or the only one like me; when I am in situations like this, that thought comes up front and center.

I think about it when I read a story of struggle like Lacey's. I think about it when members of our community call me about going back to church after having not gone for years. A woman would like to go, but she hesitates. She is worried about feeling strange, not being accepted. To take that first step is difficult, almost impossible for some. Sometimes if I accompany the woman to church, that seems to help. One woman even told me, "I would never go by myself to a church." Yet she went with me. Even so, there was still a nagging in the back of her head. She doubted her acceptance. She told herself, "If someone looks at me funny, I am outta here." Sometimes when I meet a lesbian couple, it is the woman who is not Catholic who feels more comfortable coming to Mass. The Catholic is restless and on guard. Watching, gaze constantly shifting, asking herself repeatedly, "Is it really OK for me to be here?" It is her partner who gives her to courage to step into the church—the church into which she was born.

Sometimes a woman who comes to church with me might notice two women holding hands or two men giving each other a peck on the cheek during the sign of peace. "Is it OK to do that here?" she asks, visibly shocked. "Is no one going to raise their eyebrows, give them a disgusted look, get up and leave, or—God forbid—go over and say something to them?" Then she realizes that no one is paying any attention to that couple. It is no big deal. It is just accepted. She breathes a sigh of relief and settles in a bit. "It is good to be here," I tell myself. "This is a sacred moment. I have the privilege of witnessing a woman finding her place, trying to feel at home in her church."

APPRECIATING

When you came, you were like red wine and honey,
And the taste of you burnt my mouth with its sweetness.
Now you are like morning bread,
Smooth and pleasant.
I hardly taste you at all for I know your savor,
But I am completely nourished.

—*Amy Lowell*

Recollections...

Retreat Journal

Anne is the one who finds our publisher for us. She sends a letter to Winnie at PenUltimate Press in October of 2011. She hears from Winnie in mid-November that she and her staff are interested in publishing our book. She sends me an e-mail about it on November 15. I am in retreat at the time. I open the e-mail on November 18 when I return from Iowa.

After reading Anne's e-mail, I have an odd feeling. I open my retreat journal and read the entry I made the day before Anne hears from Winnie.

The reading I pray over is from Luke's Gospel, the reading about the blind beggar. It is the reading of the day from the lectionary. I enter into the reading as though I am a beggar, and I interact with Jesus. Here is my prayer over this reading:

Alone and away from the crowd

I sit by the roadside

I hear that Jesus

Is passing by.

I get up

And go to him

Winding my way

Through the crowd

Around him.

Our eyes meet

And he calls me to him.

"What do you want me to do for you?" he asks.

"I don't know what to ask for," I say.

"Just say the word," he replies.

"To publish the book

To give a voice to others

To find my voice as well."

He touches my mouth

And takes my hands

Into his own.

We gaze at each other.
He lets go of my hands
And he walks away.

As I try to enter into this reading I wonder what to ask for. The book seemed so small a request—perhaps not appropriate—sight, insight, wisdom, seemed like so much more. But as I picture it unfolding that is what I asked for and it feels right. And it is asking for more—to have a voice. I need also the courage and calm to deal with the consequences. Jesus's gaze provides that.

Reading this journal entry, I am reminded again of our authors, women gathering in living rooms, speaking our truth, praying together, sensing that what we are doing is sacred, feeling affirmed by one another and the presence of the Divine, finding the courage to go on, to come out, to be ourselves more fully, to witness to the grace in our midst.

Coming Home

Beth Trouy

Beth loves to immerse herself in a good book, movie, or musical any chance she gets. Her friends would say she's an avid exerciser, but Beth will tell you she stays in shape only to be able to indulge in her real passion—eating! A hopeless nature and animal lover, she has a special admiration for America's national parks. She's seen eighteen so far and hopes to make it to all fifty-seven in her lifetime.

I'm a cradle Catholic, lifelong Memphian, and a product of the Catholic school system from first grade through college. I'm the youngest of four: my siblings are all boys. My entire family remains here in the Memphis area. My parents instilled in us a strong faith foundation in the church and in prayer. They lived their faith with conviction and continue today to be actively involved in the Catholic Church. As a child, I often saw my mom deep in prayer. I could see the peace in her, and it had a lasting impression on me. This feeling of peace was "home" to me.

My earliest recollection of being different was probably in junior high. I no longer felt at home with my friends at school or my family. I was an outsider: I could feel it on the inside. No one really knew me, and I couldn't open up to anyone. My initial response was one of guilt and shame for feeling what I felt inside. I tried to compensate for this evil within me by being the best, most studious, obedient person on the outside. My duplicitous Jekyll-and-Hyde life began as early as eighth grade. On the outside, I was the straight A, perfect attendance student and athlete involved in church; on the inside, I hated myself. I hated the dark side, the secret me. After all, according to what my faith, my friends, even my family told me, I was going to hell. As my self-hatred worsened, my outward perfectionism also intensified. I was running faster and faster away from the evil inside, and yet it was overtaking me. I completely understand how seemingly fine, upstanding people do horrible things; you can't live your life as two people, as a lie, and think that something is not going to explode sometime. I was wearing down and exhausted, and deep depression had set in by my sophomore year in high school. And yet I kept working harder to overcome this defect I had. I kept hoping that if I were just good enough, successful enough, smart enough, my merits would cancel out the bad in me—should it ever be discovered. Oh how I hoped it wouldn't be! I was terrified of being exposed, singled out as one of "them." I'd heard enough times in school what "they" were called and how "they" were treated differently. I'd even participated in the name-calling to further cover myself.

I was valedictorian of my class. My classmates voted me as most athletic and best all-around in our senior hall of fame. I was offered an appointment to the United States Air Force Academy (USAFA) by Senator Al Gore. I was the perfect role model for my school. In my senior year, our school worked for and achieved a national "Exemplary School Rating." This was a huge achievement for any school. Our principal asked all students to write an essay on what our school meant to us. My essay won. I read it in front of the student body, teachers, principal, bishop, and mayor of Memphis. I spoke about our rich diversity, how we were a family composed of many differing backgrounds: rich, poor, black, and white. Our school was fairly unique in that it was truly a near-equal mix of races, and I liked that. I was proud of how we respected and accepted each other's differences. I spoke of how we used those differences to make us stronger as one family. I talked of how this best prepared us for the real world. I was telling the truth as far as race relations and socioeconomic backgrounds were concerned. In my heart, it was merely a hope for what I wanted most of all: just to be accepted in spite of *my* difference. Just to be able to be fully myself and still be loved. Just to feel that peaceful feeling inside of home again. If only they knew.

As a Catholic, I knew suicide was a sin: a sure way to hell. But I thought about it more and more as I felt more trapped, backed into a corner. If I was going to hell anyway, what did it matter? At least I could spare my family, friends, and myself the pain and humiliation of what I was. I began to view dying as a relief. I was so tired. Hiding for so long and working so hard to change what I could not change had exhausted me and left me hopeless. One night, I recall the exact moment I made the shift from wanting to live to wanting to die. I had given up. I was ready to end the futility of trying to be good when I was innately flawed, bad, evil. As I visualized the steps of killing myself, I heard a voice say, "I made you in my image, and I love you just the way you are." God loves me? But everyone else has told me I was going to hell. How could God love me? But God said again, "I love you." I paused and let the "if/then proof" set in. If God loves me, then… then I am good. If God loves me then the world has been lying to me all along, all in the name of God! God never left me. God always loved me. God made me perfectly in God's image! Relief sank in and stayed but a moment when *anger* took its place—and stayed for years. These people—my family, friends, the church that I loved—had nearly pushed me to death! HOW DARE THEY!

I stopped going to church. How could I go there when I knew how they felt? What was once a peaceful refuge was now hostile territory. They say "bitterness is a poison pill you swallow yourself, hoping it will kill someone else." Anger had taken hold of me. My heart was so consumed with bitterness, I had no room for love. It took me years to see that I had only stepped down to the very level of those who'd judged me. I was nothing more than a hypocrite in shunning those who'd first shunned me. This is not what my parents, my Lord, had taught me. I was more lost than I'd ever been in my life. I knew in my heart I was wrong, and I had to forgive. It took years before I was ready. I first went back to other churches. I tried the Episcopal, Methodist, Lutheran, Presbyterian, Unitarian, and Southern Baptist denominations. I even went to First Congo and enjoyed being accepted for who I was; this was a new feeling to be in God's house and openly gay at the same time! But something was still missing. It was more than just being accepted for who I was. I missed the rosary, the stations of the cross, the sacraments; I missed the Eucharist. I began to understand that being Catholic was as much a part of me as my genetic family. In some ways I felt married to the church—and divorce was not an option. After all, I was still in love. I still loved her, even if she did not love me. The church was my home. But how could I forgive?

I recall being in my home church many years back, having a bad day, and looking up at the man who was having a worse day than me. Recently, in a bible study class, the topic of the suffering image of Jesus on the cross came up. Why, other religions ask, would the Catholic Church choose Jesus's worst moment as their symbol? Why not the empty cross of the resurrected, victorious Christ? I thought of the image of Jesus having his worst day, looking down at me with his broken body. In my suffering, I could hear Him saying, "I know how you feel." I could see Him looking at me with love all the way to his last breath. He never rejected the people—us—who nailed Him to that cross. I knew I had to go back to my faith. Not just for my sake, and not for the church's, but because of the man on the cross who loves me still. Isn't that what He calls us all to do? "Pick up your cross and follow me."

Gandhi said, "You have to be the change you want to see." Jesus said, "Love those who persecute you, do good to those who hate you." God was calling me home. After five years, I walked back into the doors of the Catholic Church with a renewed, forgiving, and thankful heart. God tells me I have every right to be here just like everyone else. Jesus never taught exclusion, only love. To my surprise, I was met with love. The Catholic Church has grown up in some areas. My bishop welcomes me; this parish welcomes me with open arms. I see Jesus here, alive! I feel I am a living viable member of a church struggling to love all at all costs as Jesus commands us.

Having a church family again gave me the courage to come out to my parents just a few years ago. It was this group, this first Tuesday potluck clan, that helped me cross that last obstacle of telling my parents they had a lesbian for a daughter. Until then, it was too much of a risk to face losing everything I considered dear to me. At least I knew I had a loving family here if my parents rejected me. But they didn't. They welcomed me with tears and open arms.

I don't get mad anymore when the closed-mindedness of others confronts me. I actually feel sorry for them that they've somehow missed out on Jesus' loving message; and I pray for them. I believe my place is here, to be me, as a living witness of the diversity of all God's people. I want to challenge some to grow and stretch their hearts out of their comfort zones and love without judging. I want to be involved in as much as I can, not necessarily with "my own kind," but with a diverse people. My high school taught me that strength lies in diversity. After all, if we remain segregated in our communities of like-mindedness, how are we ever going to accept each other's differences? How will we ever overcome our fear, our ignorance, our exclusionary laws that continue to discriminate unjustly?

I'm not afraid anymore. I feel blessed to be the whole person God made me to be in God's own image. That's something to be proud of...and I know I will never be abandoned. A verse that stuck with me from that life-changing night many years ago and still inspires me on my journey today is from Paul's letter to the Romans chapter 8:

"For I am convinced that neither death, nor life, nor angels, nor principalities, nor present things, nor future things, nor powers, nor height, nor depth, nor any other creature will be able to separate us from the love of God in Christ Jesus our Lord."

The Eighth Gift of the Holy Spirit: Diversity

Anne Boettcher

Anne is a native Wisconsinite with a strong aversion to cold and snow. Thus, this sun lover and her partner have lived for the past six years in Tucson, AZ. Weekends find them hiking nearby desert trails in sacred communion with rocks, saguaros, lizards, and hummingbirds.

This morning as I woke up and lay in bed for a while thinking about writing this reflection…a mourning dove started cooing outside my window and my partner, Mary, still mostly asleep, reached for my hand. Once again, as I often do, I thanked God for making me a lesbian.

As I look back over my life, I see God's hand unfailingly leading me to this place where I can be thankful for who I am. From my family who instilled in me a deep faith in God as well as a sense of living true to one's beliefs and accepting others, even if they were different from one's self…to the Catholic Sisters of my childhood and young adulthood who gave me a strong sense of myself as an independent and capable woman…to both of the Catholic colleges I attended where first my mind and then my whole being were opened up to new ideas and ways of relating to God and the world…to the Catholic high school in which I taught theology for sixteen years and the freedom I was given to explore hot topics and vital life issues with my students…to my friends who supported my coming-out process and my therapist, Helen, who moved my process forward by leaps and bounds…to the older Catholic Sisters of my post-teaching career who mostly unknowingly, but still lovingly, brought Mary and me together and encouraged us in our relationship with them and each other…to Mary herself, who is the love of my life, an ongoing source of inspiration and joy and a constant living, breathing, laughing, and loving revelation of God who is Love.

I feel badly for so many of my lesbian sisters who have felt the need to leave their faith and conscious connection to God behind in order to explore their sexuality. Often they are only able to return to a relationship with God years down the road. I feel very blessed to have never had my conscious connection with God broken and to know in my soul that it is God who has lead me to the truth about my sexual orientation.

While I've never lost my God-connection, I am very angry because the Catholic hierarchy consistently closes the windows on Vatican II and the changes that might have stretched the church to include even the likes of me—a woman for starters, and then a sexually active lesbian in a committed relationship. I have experienced several Catholic communities that have been wonderfully welcoming and accepting. Still I can't seem to get beyond the anger I feel because the old boys' club at the top restricts the participation of more than half its members solely based on physical anatomy—and then outright condemns a different, but overlapping, segment of humanity because we are true to the Spirit within us and love who we love. The recovery work I've done tells me I'm enabling the system by warming a pew on Sunday. And to extend that analogy, an intervention of epic proportions needs to take place before I can feel like I'm not compromising my own recovery by joining the family at the table. In my opinion, too many of the folks at the Sunday table enable and support the dysfunction, giving priest, bishop, cardinal, and pope way too much power. I love my mom and dad very much, and they've become two of Mary's and my best supports. Yet, when I first came out to them eight years ago, it took two years of uncomfortable silences before my parents finally faced their fears for my soul and went and talked to their parish priest. Thank God, Father was an enlightened priest, and he helped my parents accept me as the good woman that they told him I was, regardless of my sexual orientation. My point is that it took only twenty minutes or so with Father to finally validate who I am. Where would I be if this priest had been conservative or even just a by-the-books kind of guy?! I greatly admire the Call to Action folks and others who try to change the church from the grassroots level, but as I see it, the Catholic Church is not a democracy—and the mode at the top for a while now has been one of entrenchment rather than listening for the Spirit moving among the folks in the pews. I can't seem to get beyond my anger to accept the nourishment offered by the Catholic community…so I leave and I grieve.

What is it that I grieve though? My parents are good, devoted, middle-of-the-road Catholics. They were raised in the church of the '40s and '50s and yet were pretty open to the changes of Vatican II. As a child in the early '60s, I was immersed in the pre-Vatican II traditions. I had my rosary that I said daily with my parents. I had quite the collection of holy cards. I loved reading stories about the lives of the saints (and it's probably pretty telling that I was especially drawn to the reformers like John of the Cross and Teresa of Avila and the ones I like to call the "transcenders," like Hildegard of Bingen, Francis of Assisi, and Julian of Norwich). Going to church on Sundays, holy days, and holidays, as well as attending Advent and Lenten devotions, gave structure and depth to our family and nurtured my spirituality. I still find myself resorting to saying the rosary in bed at night when I can't sleep (changing the "thee's" and "thou's" as well as omitting the "sinners"—I'm a compulsive prayer translator!). I find that the rhythm and the familiarity soothe me. When it's adapted to account for evolving times and circumstances (as Vatican II started to do), the Catholic tradition is a rich resource.

The second aspect I value and miss is the Catholic sense of sacrament. To be introduced to and adopted by a faith community as an infant, then to learn about, freely commit to, and be recognized as a responsible and respected member of that same community as one reaches adulthood can be a profound affirmation of the key transitions in one's life. To be able to go to one's peers, or their appointed and trained representative, and to be ritually forgiven for one's mistakes and challenged and supported to grow, can be a wonderful gift. To gather as a community around the table on a regular basis to be both inspired and nourished can be a powerful experience of the Divine Essence that unites and gives life to us all. I know that other denominations also celebrate sacraments but somehow, so far, it's not the same.

The final thing that comes to mind when I think about what I grieve is community. Being Catholic was a big part of my identity and my sense of belonging for most of my life. Between my parish and the Catholic high school where I taught—and the good friends I'd made along the way in both places—my context was pretty much the Catholic Church. I also knew that wherever I went, be it Ireland, Honduras, or just another city, I could and did find a Mass somewhere and felt at least a small connection to my spiritual home. As I've felt more and more alienated from the church, I've definitely lost a lot of that sense of belonging.

So what have I found to nurture my spirit and how does being a lesbian affect my relationship with the Divine Essence? My awareness runs along Trinitarian lines. God as Creator is huge for both Mary and me. Getting out hiking in the desert of southern Arizona where we live is wonderful for my soul. Each saguaro cactus speaks to me of a life of standing in faithfulness to the sun and its life-giving light. The hummingbirds remind me to be thankful for the sweetness and time for play with which I've been blessed. The coyote chorus singing in the night calls me beyond fear of the unknown. The dry heat comfortably baking my bones moves me to awareness of God's love surrounding and enveloping me in much the same way. The sense of both my strength and sometimes my breathlessness as I climb the mountain trails reminds me that I am wonderfully made. Being in touch with my sensual being seems intimately linked to my sexuality and nurtures my spirituality.

Secondly, being a member of an oppressed minority gives me an enhanced appreciation for Jesus—who spent a lot of his time with the outcasts and so-called sinners; who challenged the unjust religious laws and structures of his time; who held the spirit of the law as more important than the letter; who cured the lepers, uplifted the poor, validated the sexually unclean—real or perceived; and who taught that God is not the ultimate judge but rather the essence of forgiving and redeeming love. There's a small part of me that wishes he would come again to clean up the church in Rome the way he did the temple in Jerusalem. Mostly though I just feel validated and humbled to know that he came to set the likes of me free from societal condemnation and oppression and from my own self-destructive responses to it. He was willing to die a horrible death rather than back down and stop preaching about the love God has for each and every one of us. I believe Jesus is bigger than any church, and his example of love and compassion, justice and forgiveness is an inspiration for any time and culture. I believe it is the Divine Essence, embodied in Jesus but also rising in each of us, that calls and empowers us to go out and follow not only his example, but also the example of other holy ones throughout the ages, allowing divine light and love to shine through our lives, our attitudes, and our actions toward others.

The third major form that my own personal trinity takes is that of Oneness. A significant reason for my moving beyond the Catholic Church has been due, not to rejection, but to the call of the Universe Story and a sense of inclusion. Throughout my years of teaching introduction to scripture courses, I presented the biblical creation stories as allegories, pointing the way to truth while not needing to be literally factual. I offered the Big Bang theory as an alternative creation story where God's essence was initiator, as well as light, energy, and ultimate life within the unfolding of the Universe. Modern day theologians and scientists refer to this creation model as the Universe Story, and it speaks to my soul. It encompasses the sense of union and oneness found within the mystical elements of spiritual traditions the world over. It provides a solid theological foundation for our current response to the ecological crisis, moving us from "man's dominion over" to a framework where humanity is part of the whole, intimately connected with the rest of creation. I think this model appeals to me especially as a lesbian because it's very inclusive. Diversity and change are the tools of the Divine One who created every body and every thing from the same stardust and Divine Energy. From this oneness we all emerge and to this oneness we all return. Each and every being—lesbian and straight;

Catholic and Buddhist; cactus, coyote, and cooing dove—is Divine Essence, embodied in an infinite variety of forms.

I believe that our diversity is a gift from God and the hope for our future. I believe that, as each of us brings unique perspectives and abilities, talents and gifts to the table—Eucharistic or otherwise—all of us are enriched. I believe that the various crises in which we find ourselves today can serve as catalysts, moving us beyond factions and prejudices to an appreciation of the contributions each one can and needs to make so all of us can survive and thrive. I believe that each of us is called to look inside ourselves, recognizing, affirming, and evolving the unique gifts that God has embodied within us.

Among the many ways God has blessed me, I thank God for making me a lesbian, with all the gifts inherent therein. These gifts especially I offer to the Divine Essence to add to the rich diversity of the Eternal One.

A Blessed Life

Anne Peper Perkins

Anne Peper Perkins is known as Granny Annie not only to her six grandchildren, but also to the many other children she knows and loves. She leads a busy life—teaching T'ai Chi Chih to young and old; making sock monkeys, candles, and quilts for friends, family, and church; doing Healing Touch and Breema on cancer patients; memorizing seventeenth-century sonnets and writing her memoir; living happily with her spouse Mary in a beautiful city neighborhood called Lafayette Square in a one-hundred-thirty-year-old Victorian house. A blessed life indeed.

How is my spirituality flourishing? Who helps me on my journey?

Oh, dear wonderful God—of Love, of Wonder, of Joy, of Surprise, of Sadness—yes, even of sadness…help me as I start to answer these questions.

I feel blessed, so very blessed: Blessed in my beloved partner Mary and in the beautiful grandchildren that we share; blessed in my three lovely adult sons and their dear spouses, and in my wonderful stepdaughter; blessed in my way-out Catholic church, which is such a haven for so many of us; blessed in so many dear friends; blessed in my Healing Touch work with cancer patients and my T'ai-Chi-Chih teaching. Blessed.

Most of my days begin with two kinds of being-with-God. When I wake up I usually have time to meditate while I am still in bed: I give myself a long Chakra Connection, part of my training as a Healing Touch practitioner. Often I find myself whispering, "Be still, and know that I am here," or simply breathing in and out slowly and with awareness. Frequently I say the prayer of St. Francis of Assisi ("Lord, make me an instrument of thy peace…") and Psalm 23 ("The Lord is my Shepherd…"), usually in Spanish because it's the language I am trying to learn. A month or so ago, I realized that I was doing way more talking to God than listening, and in those precious moments of silent listening I heard the words "Rest on me, child." So now I have incorporated that invitation into my morning meditation and feel God's comforting presence even more.

The second kind of being-with-God is more communal: most days I attend the early-morning service at my parish church. Usually our pastor says Mass, though on Tuesdays there is normally a Communion service presided over by Sharon, a lovely woman who, with Marge, first helped to gather and organize our lesbian storytellers. Sharon was educated at Eden Theological Seminary in St. Louis and listens closely to the insights of her heart; after the service I do a special bodywork called Breema on her, and that seems to extend the sacredness of the time for both of us. Sometimes my dear friend Sr. Leah, a Daughter of Charity who works in the nearby health clinic, leads the Communion service; her gentle and wise soul is a gift to us all. Our daily church community is tiny, united by our delight in the liturgy and by our eagerness to hear and share the Scriptures with each other (our pastor, Sharon and Sr. Leah encourage all of us to contribute our thoughts to a kind of communal homily). We bring our prayers for the coming of peace and social justice; for the sick, the depressed, and the marginalized; and for our families and close friends who are in need. Nearly always we gather around the altar as the prayers of the consecration are said. At the end of the Communion service, we always say what we are grateful for, and our thanks move freely, for example, from the children in our lives, to an autumn walk in the park, to the many people in our lives who support us.

My parish church remains the foundation of my communal faith-life these days. I started attending services there nearly thirteen years ago, and I often say to friends and family that this is the church I have looked for all my life. And it is! I absolutely love the 10 a.m. liturgy on Sundays—its exuberance, in particular—and I love that my youngest grandson Benjy shares my enthusiasm. At nine and a half years old, he has spent nearly every Saturday night with Mary and me for more than two years (he lives in Springfield, Illinois, about an hour and a half away), and he truly loves coming to church with me. There is a good possibility that he will make his First Communion this coming spring, though I have been very unwilling to push it in any way (my oldest son Jonathan and daughter-in-law Vicki, both raised Catholic and now quite negative about the church, have nevertheless been completely gracious and loving about my taking Benjy with me every Sunday). I admit that it would be a great joy to have him become a communicant in the church community he loves so much.

For many years I have been involved with children's Liturgy of the Word in my parish; I especially love praying with the six-to-ten year olds—including, of course, the marvelous children of the lesbian couples who have been so welcomed over the years by the parish. I feel that I learn so much from so many of the children: very recently, for example, one youngster referred to Jesus as the Love King! I have also become the unofficial candle maker for the various feasts and seasons, and I love seeing my many-layered soy candles on the altar. And I have been involved with the liturgy committee as well, sometimes helping with Advent and Lent vespers, occasionally writing the prayers of the faithful, and participating in decorating the church for special feasts. I am also an eager lector, and my pleasure in it reminds me of my dear mother, who loved reading aloud at church in her beautifully clear and intelligent voice (she converted from Presbyterianism to Roman Catholicism about eighteen years after she and my father were married). I love the women's retreats we have once or twice a year, and I love offering T'ai Chi Chih during them. All of these activities help me to feel grounded in, and cherished by, this particular community—a wonderfully eccentric community marked by loving inclusiveness. And week after week, the community of preachers—both men and women, lay and religious—constantly challenges me to think in terms of social justice, something that I was almost completely unaware of before becoming a part of this parish. In the last couple of years, led by three women in particular, we as a parish have been welcoming an increasing number of the neighborhood children who attend Mass on Sundays without their parents: some play drums or sing in the choir; some are being tutored after Mass; many stay afterward for juice and donuts and have a play period with Maria; all are being hugged and loved by many of us, and we by them in return. Right now several of us are trying to get Lamont, a fourteen-year-old boy from the neighborhood, into a local Catholic school where he will be safer and encouraged to nurture his interest in writing.

It is not just my church community that nourishes my spirituality. I am also intensely involved with three activities, all of which I have mentioned above. I am an accredited Healing Touch practitioner, and as I continue to work with family and friends, I receive such affirmation of the spiritual blessings of this particular form of "energy work"—spiritual blessings for both the giver and the receiver. I have a massage table at home, and there are three friends who come regularly to me—all suffer from serious diseases (metastasized cancer, Crohn's disease), and they have told me that they find comfort in our sessions. I also work with cancer patients at Hope Lodge, a residence hall run by the American Cancer Society where people can live free of charge as they undergo radiation and chemotherapy. I started a volunteer program there nearly eight years ago, and three of us take turns offering free Healing Touch sessions on Thursday afternoons. It was several years ago when I was at Hope Lodge that I had an experience of a sacred Presence: I was at the patient's head, holding his shoulders lightly at first, then moving down towards the arms. Suddenly I felt myself being held by huge arms. I realized that both of us were being held, and that I had simply become the vehicle by which the patient was being embraced by a divine presence.

I am also a certified practitioner of Breema, and I work on several friends regularly (particularly my friend Sharon, as I mentioned above). This is a form of bodywork where gentle brushes, easy stretches, and tender holds nourish both the receiver and the giver.

After I receive a Breema treatment I often say, "That's as close to Heaven as I get on this earth!" The bodywork, however, is really just an excuse to practice the nine principles of Breema, principles like "Single Moment, Single Activity," "No Force," "Full Participation." These principles in turn lead to a kind of meditative stance towards everything the practitioner does in her/his life, because they encourage an awareness of, and reverence towards, the present moment—where we are most likely to encounter God.

And this brings me to T'ai Chi Chih (hereafter, TCC), the third activity nurturing my spiritual life. I have practiced TCC for more than twelve years, almost every day, and have been an accredited teacher for about nine years. TCC is called a "moving meditation," and over the years it has softened and slowed me down (something I still need more of!). And my TCC teaching has really blossomed in the past year and a half, when I have been volunteering at a marvelous parochial school in the city. I have twelve different groups of children, from the kindergartners through the eighth grade (in the sixth, seventh, and eighth grades, the children are divided by gender), and I see them each for about fifteen minutes every Tuesday. They seem to love it, and I certainly do too! Last year, about a month after I had first come to the school, the school principal, Sr. Gail Tippett, took part in a practice with the eighth-grade boys who, up until then, had been the opposite of cooperative. We were outside in the side yard, and at the end of what was a beautifully quiet session, she said to them so earnestly, "Gentleman, today you have showed us your souls." Then at the beginning of this year, when I asked the present eighth-grade boys (as seventh graders last year they were one of my most eager classes) to explain TCC to the three or four new students in the class, a lovely tall boy in the back raised his hand and said so solemnly, "It's all about peace and tranquility." And it is. And it is wonderful that many of the young students, and some of their teachers, understand that. I also do TCC every week with two other groups and have done so for many years: I work with older women at Alexian Brothers P.A.C.E. (Program of All-Inclusive Care for the Elderly), where even those in wheelchairs can and do take part (recently three marvelous Vietnamese women have joined P.A.C.E and our TCC group); I also lead a group of parishioners before the 10 a.m. Sunday liturgy at my parish church. And so I am involved with the very young and the very old and the medium, and I love all these roles.

But now to the people in my life who especially nurture my spirituality:

First of all, my dear spouse Mary, who continually amazes me with the extraordinary scope of her studies and pursuits (everything from studying quantum physics and ancient

Egyptian hieroglyphs to playing Broadway songs on the piano, all in the past few years).
We have been together for almost twenty years (starting when I was forty-nine and she was
fifty-eight years old), and they have been remarkably full and exciting years together. Her
story is a complex one, but suffice it to say here that she is the one who helped me to fully
recognize my bi-sexuality. Mary was raised by an Episcopalian mother and tried coming to
my parish a few times, but she simply does not believe in Christianity, particularly Roman
Catholicism. She believes in the truth of the universal compassion of the Buddhists, but
also, unlike a Buddhist, believes in God. And yet her God is a God of love, and beauty,
and understanding, rather than a God who is the creator of the universe. She admires
Jesus very much, particularly his radical "Love your enemies," and she is sharply critical
of the fact that the Christian creed leaves out Jesus' life of love and concentrates on his
miraculous birth and suffering death and resurrection (as she puts it, "It is a church that
worships power, not love."). We talk about religion fairly frequently, and she constantly
challenges my beliefs (and I often feel wishy-washy when talking to her). Although she
is very negative about the Roman Catholic Church, and especially the hierarchy, she
admires my parish community and is enormously supportive of my involvement there.
Her absolute love for me holds me in a grounding embrace, and in that way she is the
primary image of God's presence of love in my life.

My friends Charlene and Jan have become my special "God-people." Charlene and I
met on jury duty twelve and a half years ago, and she also attends my parish church. We
have spent many hours walking together in Tower Grove Park and the Botanical Garden,
talking about God and prayer, discussing poetry and teaching. She is constantly giving
me books; she breaks into prayer, whether on the phone or on a walk or at church after a
service; she strongly encourages me to write in my journal. When one of us is consider-
ing some new decision in our lives, Charlene often asks "What gives you life?" and I often
counter with my own phrase, "What is the loving thing to do?" My friend Jan and I met
about two and a half years ago, when she started going to my parish church; she is the
person who is probably the most responsible for encouraging me to have a regular
meditation time. Although accompanying her husband as he is slowly dying of complications from Alzheimer's disease, she herself gets up at about 6 a.m. each morning, and
"sits with God." Now I find myself longing to have that early morning time, that quiet
peace, that Jan so beautifully exemplifies. About a year ago she suggested starting a prayer
group, and now five of us gather about once a month to pray with poetry (the hostess gets
to choose the poems—often by Mary Oliver—for the meeting). I am so grateful that Jan

came into my life when she did. And so grateful that I have the grace of these two women to be such loving and prayerful companions on my faith journey.

And of course there are important others who nourish my spirituality. My friend Terri's deep love and constant acceptance have moved me towards far greater self-confidence in the nearly twenty-five years I have known her. My psychotherapist Anne D. constantly moves me gently towards greater self-awareness. My middle son Andrew is a model of gentleness and kindness, despite the tragic drowning of his sweetheart right before his eyes in the summer of 1999. My youngest son Ben, who so delights in his role as father, is also dedicated to social justice (and he's the one who first introduced me to Mary Oliver's poetry!). My ninety-seven-year-old father prays on his knees every morning and evening for others by name, mostly for those who used to be Catholics to return to the church, or for those who have died to get to Heaven (ah well, you can see that my father is a somewhat exasperating nurturer of my spirituality!). And although I have not been actively going to Al-Anon meetings in the past year and a half, there are many, many twelve-step friends who have influenced me in the past, a number of whom continue to encourage me right now to speak the truth more clearly, to love and cherish kindness over "niceness," and to take better care of myself. I always say that twenty-five years ago my epitaph would have read, "She helped a lot"; then it changed to "She loved a lot"; now it is "She enjoyed a lot." And I feel strongly that the last includes the two earlier ones.

Which brings me, after all these wonderfully positive paragraphs listing my many blessings and supporters, to another question: what do I want and need more of in my life? First of all, I yearn for more quiet time with God. More meditation, more praying, less running around "doing good," more real loving. It is very hard for me to slow down, because I love my life, love the activities that I do, love being with others. A few days ago I read that all of life can be lived as if in meditation. And I love Elizabeth Ann Seton's words, "We must pray literally without ceasing, I mean that prayer of the heart which is independent of time and place, which is rather a habit of lifting up the heart to God." So perhaps I can still be busy, and yet also be in prayerful, contemplative mode as well? Or is this just an excuse? I do know that I often feel overextended these days…

"Oh God, help me to love."

"Oh God, help me."

"Oh God!"

"Rest on me, child."

Amen. And alleluia.

A couple of months after I wrote the above, I found yet another phrase which I love dearly and now use very often during my meditations: "Fold the wings of your mind, and bring your mind into your heart."

Heading Home

Alice F. Hoenigman

Alice is a strong woman, a partner, sister, writer, student, and an e-bay seller. She's a married wom-
an according to her and her family, though she's waiting on that recognition from her state. She is
gregarious. She enjoys politics and sports. Alice is a dog-lover, traveler, and martial artist. She's a
hands-on aunt. She lives in Indianapolis, but she'll always be a Clevelander. She's the child of Ed
and Ann, very wise parents.

Let me make it clear to the world…I'm not into retreats. My dear friend said she would
be thinking of me, because my weekend sounded like it was going to be merciless; other
friends said goodbye as if I were dying. My favorite response was "a Catholic, gay retreat,
isn't that an oxymoron?" However, my wife and I kept an open mind…well, most of the
time we did. There were at least two rounds of her wanting to bail and then my wanting
to bail, but we talked each other back into it. God made it so one of us was strong at the
other's hour (or hours) of bail.

It had been the culmination of four years of discomfort between my parents on the one
hand, and me and my partner on the other. We had just begun to stabilize our relationship with my parents, so the thought of her mother, my parents, and us in the woods for a
weekend sounded like it could turn quickly into the WWF (World Wrestling Federation) of
Catholicism. Of course, Audry and I were not the ones in the ring, but we were the reason
for the ring; then again, we're used to that. The olive branch was being offered, but we
were so scared to take it, coming as it was after the dark years. It wasn't that my parents did
not like Audry; it's that they didn't know her—which is fine for a one-year relationship, but
when you're approaching four years and you're engaged, something had to give.

I had worked with a group of women on handling these four difficult years because
my family is very important to me. But so is Audry. The women I worked with helped me
to develop patience. I would go home to Cleveland for holidays year after year without
Audry, not to be a martyr, not to minimize her role in my life; I would do it because I
realized that even though I was the young one, the baby of the family, the college kid, I
had to be mature on this one, serious mature, bullshit mature, grown-up mature. I had to
be the bigger person, I had to come home without my partner holiday after holiday and
not be punishing about it. That would only make it harder to rebuild when it was time.

There are a lot of things my parents did that they regret. As most queer people say, it was the same-sex parent who was the most difficult. For me, this was my mother. She did things I know weren't characteristic of her, but the fear that having a gay daughter brings to an old Irish Catholic mother—well, it was just too much. I am the youngest of six kids and grew up in Cleveland, Ohio. I was living in Dayton, Ohio, at this point, and was a junior in college. I think that when I started college, my parents had the feeling they were finally "done"—all the kids were out of the home, in school, or graduated from school. And then boom, I come home with that conversation that is so hard to have and represents the beginning, not the end, of that experience. So, to briefly explain, my parents were supportive of me from the second I said those words to them. But to clarify what, I believe, may be a misconception: There are not two responses only when you deliver that news: good or bad, supportive or unsupportive. My parents were always supportive, but we also had major issues: those responses are not mutually exclusive. I remember my mother telling me that I looked like a boy, being rude to gender-queer friends, and telling me that I was embarrassing. I remember two bad fights, one resulting in a scene with my father and sister trying to calm me while I sat on our washing machine, crying tears like a baby while punching the walls like a man. I remember my mom getting disproportionately mad when I didn't get my sister a present for her wedding shower (what lesbian is into wedding shower gifts?). The reason she was mad was that my sister wanted me to bring Audry to the wedding, and my mother was furious; it wasn't ever about the towel set. I remember bad things, but just barely.

That wedding was a major turning point for my mother, because Audry attended it with me. We were both scared, but we were also focused. It was the first time Audry had been at my parents' house. We slept in twin beds in the attic. Audry lay down in her bed; it squeaked loudly, and she said in the dark, "oh…Catholic beds." We howled. Sometimes the smallest thing will make you feel in your element, even when you're not. We stayed calm that weekend, we prayed a lot, and we stayed near my two very supportive sisters. My sisters have shared this experience, and they have their own scars from defending me.

During that wedding weekend, I felt like my mother finally realized Audry wasn't a monster or a heathen or both; she was just a woman, a person, a college kid. I think my mother also realized how much happier I seemed when Audry was around. Things changed, slowly at first, but they changed. That Christmas my mom asked me to bring Audry home to Cleveland. Cards started to have Audry's name on them too. The phone goodbye now included, "give my best to Audry." It was still touchy—don't get me wrong—but at least we were trying.

So I got the call from my mother about the retreat, with an accompanying flier in the mail from my dad. Well…shit. I don't see how there's any getting out of this one. The whole time that I'd been out to my parents, they were attending a parents-of-gays support group at a Catholic church in Cleveland. My parents are not just a little bit Catholic; let me be clear. My father goes to church every day; volunteers for a million different causes; donates his money, time, and skills to the church. My mother dragged all six of us kids to church every Sunday. It was like herding chickens, I'm sure, but she was committed, and she has a big net. My mother makes sense of the world though her spirituality. She is also a card-carrying Democrat, and her politics meld into her spirituality sometimes. I am just like my mother. We are loud; we can sit at any table and have friends. We are storytellers, Democrats, baseball fans, and writers. We are so much alike, we just have to laugh. My mom did understand not to push me on the Catholic thing since I came out. Even in the dark years, my parents were furious at the church about its handling or not handling of gay, lesbian, bisexual, and transgendered (GLBT) church members and their parents. I remember when the priest sex abuse scandal hit, and the Vatican said gay men might not be able to be priests. My dad said if that happened he'd leave the church, and when he said that, our loud, big, high-volume family was stunned silent.

So, the flier and the phone call say the same thing: My parents are inviting Audry, me, and Audry's parents to come with them to a retreat through their parents-of-gays support group at St. John Vianney parish in Cleveland. Audry heard the word. I admire her strength: she said a strong "yes," and delighted in inviting her mother and father to come from Cincinnati. She encouraged me by this example. She is a brave woman. So, the weekend came. It was an October weekend in Cleveland, which means the leaves are beginning to turn, there is a tiny chill in the air, and nights begin to get cold. We had made it to the retreat house, a four-hour drive from our university apartment, and were back home again in Cleveland, nervous.

The first person we saw upon arriving was Audry's mother, Nancy. Her father was unable to make the retreat, so her brave mother came alone. She drove five hours to get to the retreat house. She had mixed feelings about my parents. She and her husband did not blink in their acceptance of their daughter. They were so exceptionally supportive of Audry and of me. They were a bit hurt by my parents' slow response to Audry. Love is protective, and her parents knew it hurt Audry that my parents didn't invite her all those holidays for all those years. I had a great relationship with Audry's parents. In four years we'd already been over all the hurdles of daughter's partner stuff, and we were close. I think my parents needed to see that though. They needed to realize that they were, in fact, behind in embracing this relationship, though we were thrilled they were trying. There are some things you cannot soften, and this was one of them. I think my mom realized, as she saw my relationship with Nancy, just how much time we had spent together and how little time my parents had spent with Audry. Nancy is a strong woman who knows forgiveness is wise. She was there, and we were grateful.

The first night was a Friday, but everyone was just getting there. My parents looked thrilled; I could tell by their faces they were pumped. We sat at dinner the first night, which was sort of the main event; most of Friday was just arriving, unpacking, and gathering for a little meet and greet. I remember feeling relieved and nervous at the same time. I found out Audry and I would be sleeping in different rooms, and that made me a bit uneasy: it felt campy (god, I hated camp), but we agreed to keep a positive attitude. I slept that night in a room with a crucifix and a picture of Jesus. It had been a long time since I'd been in this type of environment, but I breathed deeply and lay down to sleep. Saturday morning came easy. I found the other smokers, I made our mothers laugh, I uncurled my toes. It was around this time that I began to feel calmer.

I met several people whose bravery made me humble. I met a lesbian couple who'd been together forty-five years, old and gray lesbians, retired lesbians, the kind that aren't really represented in the gay trendy spots in the cities I'd lived. I wanted to know every detail of their existence. I wondered if they'd think my generation is soft; they acknowledged that, in any generation, this stuff is hard. I connected most with Winnie; she was so happy to see the "young ones." I felt the same way about seeing her there. There is something about seeing that a person who looks just like you do preceded you; it confirms that others will come after you.

I would meet up with Audry after sessions, and she would be glowing. Sometimes she was with my parents in a session, sometimes she wasn't, but she was having a good time. Her face was relaxed.

I took to private reflection in my room. I could see the sun shining in through the window. The tile under my feet felt cold and solid. I thought about all the things that had led up to this moment. The bad dates with bad people, the hidden Lesbian Resource Book in my bedroom when I was seventeen, the tattooed butch who cut my hair short for the first time in her basement, the panic attacks, the dyke bars, the trips home, the love of my life. This was a sacred moment—my life had clicked. Who would've thought five years ago that this would occur at a Catholic retreat? But it did, undeniably.

I went to dinner that night feeling calm and content. My parents were talking to my mother-in-law, which made Audry and me squeeze each other's hands under the table. They were clicking, we always knew they would if they'd only get the chance. Each time we looked up they were laughing together—heads back, belly laughing. Audry looked at me and shook her head; it was incredible to see this happen.

Saturday night we were going to have confession and some type of long church-centered evening. I was OK with that, but not ecstatic. So we sat in the chapel: natural sunlight poured in at the start of Mass. My hands were sweaty; it had been a while. I listened to the words of the readings given in inclusive language. I listened about god as "god," not as "he." I heard guitar strings vibrate and recognized the same black music stands that we used in my Catholic elementary school. I watched the little flames of the candles dance. When the sign of peace was exchanged, I hugged the people around me as if I'd known them for years. I watched my parents embrace Nancy; I kissed my wife-to-be.

Then, round two: confession. The facilitators had given everyone colored pieces of paper. We were instructed to write some behaviors or traits we were either not proud of or sorry for. I thought this was cool. I remember staring at those papers for a long time before writing. It is hard to see your shortcomings written down. It was powerful. The priest said to tear up all the pieces of colored paper, get rid of the emotional baggage, the anger or sadness we felt. A nonverbal, nontraditional way of going to confession. There was a small table in the center of the room. We were each to go up to the front of the room and scatter our small pieces of paper. A symbolic cleansing, taking away the power of our mistakes, egos, and anger. I loved this.

There was also traditional confession, which I did not participate in; it seemed a strange gesture for me that I wasn't quite ready for. Catholic school had been rough turf for a stone butch. Teachers ignored insults, threats to my person were minimized and ignored, priests and nuns had treated me badly—not all, but enough that I still contract a bit until I know them. And of course, that ever-educational religion class video, "My Buddy's Gay." So, retreat I was ready for; confession, not a chance. I watched as other people got in line and confessed. I felt peaceful and relaxed.

I caught my mother in my line of sight, walking up to the table with her colored scraps of paper. I was watching her, thinking about her. My mother—she is such a storyteller, so gregarious, full of wit. She always brought down the house with her humor. I saw her with her scraps of paper listing the shortcomings and qualities that she regretted. She dropped them onto the center table, but she kept some of the scraps in her hand. I was curious about what she was doing. Before I could figure it out, she was one step in front of me. She did not look at me. She dropped her papers at my feet, touched my shoulder, and sat back down. The message was clear: my mother was apologizing. Tears ran down my face. Audry held my hand. Audry had been alongside me during the storms and crashes. She felt for a time as I did that it wouldn't change. The light would not come. As we sat in this makeshift chapel in the woods outside my hometown, my mother had, without question, without prompting, apologized. And she had done it in a way true to herself—not in a letter or a card (she wasn't a card person), not with a drawn-out lengthy address, but in a gesture. It was and is the most powerful gesture I've ever seen or received. We never talked about it again.

Then I remember feeling a tap on my leg and looking up to see my mother. She looked mischievous and pointed towards the door. We made our escape into the night as a line formed for those who wished to make the traditional confession. We got outside, and I said, "What are we doing?" She asked me for a cigarette, which she only did on very special occasions. She pulled from her purse what I least expected, some small bottles of wine. She said, "It was getting too long in there, and I know you're not into confession. I figured we could just hang out and talk until everyone gets out. I brought you some wine." I laughed out loud. My sneaky mother. She follows the rules but certainly bends them; she jokes about her attention span and talks about how, if church gets too long or too history-driven, she can't hang with it. She moves me along in my stories if she feels I'm getting too windy. She gets away with it. Her charm is unmatched; her wit is unrelenting. She was always the parent who came up with the best ideas of what to do on a summer day. She always identifies with the one sitting out back, telling stories instead of being in school, and here we were doing that again, me in my early twenties, her in her early sixties. We talked easily and simply. We laughed from our guts. Amid sips of red wine we took in the world around us under the bright stars and in the cold air. It was all so easy. It reminded me of the timelessness of my relationship with my mother. Her hands just the same as they were when I'd hold them as a child; her laugh as familiar as my own reflection; her voice; her hair; her winter coat. Nothing was different, no one had scars; it was simple and true. I believe that will always be one of the most important moments of my life. I remember only vaguely what we talked about, but it was never about that. It was the gesture, the moment in time, that was ours. Only my mother could make amends by sneaking wine into a church retreat, and a GAY retreat, no less! Style and grace. One by one our forgiven friends trickled out. They joined in our conversations; they laughed at the trafficked wine; they joked that my mother needed a bigger suitcase.

I got married to Audry a year later. My parents walked me down the aisle. My parents do not tolerate me…they adore me…and I them.

Reflections...

The Gifts We Offer

I have attended numerous workshops about lesbian, gay, bisexual, and transgendered ministry and concerns. I have had hundreds of conversations with individuals and groups of gay men and lesbian women. Often we talk about issues regarding church and our community, and so many conversations sound similar. It is not unusual for a group to talk about the gifts they have to offer the church. I find it touching to hear gay men and lesbian women and parents of both offering their gifts to our faith community. These conversations have been deeply *reflective* and spiritually rich.

I hear our women saying these same things as well, through their writings. At our meetings as we share what we have written, I hear their pride and commitment. They know they have much to offer their faith community. When we come together, we are deeply reflective. We speak in ways that I don't hear straight or heterosexual Catholics speak. Heterosexuals don't know how to answer a question like, "When did you first realize you were straight?"

I invite you to continue listening with an inner ear to these stories. Reflect on your life. Have you ever thought about this? Do you worry about that? Let us listen in....

Our women talk about how they realized at an early age that they were different. For most it was a difficult truth to bear, as Beth made clear when she talked about being an outsider at school and even in her family.

Like Beth, others tell me of their awareness of the blessing of God in their lives and of God's warm and healing acceptance. Coming to self-acceptance, feeling affirmed, and developing a conviction that this is right, "It is who I am." They come to see their inner *journey as sacred.*

In preparing for the publication of this book, I read each piece dozens of times. I found myself taking notes and jotting down feeling phrases. Finally I decided to count the feelings I found to see what I would discover. I soon abandoned pen and paper and began recording them on the computer. In the end, I had a list of more than one hundred phrases. Then I divided them into what seemed like positive and negative feelings. To my surprise, the positive feelings outnumber the negative ones two to one.

Looking at my page on the computer, I see both the pain and the joy of our writers. I also get a sense of the journey and feel the strength and courage they have as they resolve their doubts, affirm themselves, and begin to live integrated lives.

I know it takes years for a woman to achieve peace of mind and heart like this. Often she comes to this through profound experiences of prayer. She finds a new image of God. She lets herself experience a loving God. She discovers that she can channel the deep longing she has in her life to God; she realizes that it is God for whom she longs. She finds unconditional love in her God. She experiences forgiveness and finds that her tears are sacramental. She might go to an empty church and find God and acceptance in the quiet darkness of that sacred space. She can go into a forest or walk along a beach and find God in nature. She begins to feel transformed; she lives a resurrected life.

As I talk with them, hear them share their stories, and pray with them, I hear an appreciation for life and an *appreciation for mystery.* Our women know that there are things they cannot explain. They accept things as they are and live with gratitude. They begin to see that they do not have to make excuses for their lives. They discover that they cannot force or compel other people to understand or accept them. They begin to let go and to give up trying to control. In this they find peace and the support of a loving God who made them and loves them for who they are.

Often, after making peace with herself and with God, a woman can also *integrate her faith and her life.* She can look at her life with new eyes and see ways to apply scripture to what is happening to her. She can also integrate her personal story with the larger, ongoing, and unfolding story of the church as a whole. She can integrate prayer and service. Anne Perkins' writing about the blessings in her life reflects this. For Anne, it is all a blessing.

Although this may not be true for everyone, much of a woman's ability to become integrated arises from *a capacity for suffering and sympathy.* Because she has experienced rejection, fear, and self-doubt. Because she has had to accept hard truths about herself. Because she feels the pain of being different. She has developed inner strength through all of this. This capacity for suffering is related to *embracing exile.* She feels like she is looking at life from the edges, the margins. She longs for a day in which our society and church can accept her more fully.

Sadly, some can't find acceptance in our church. Anne Boetcher writes about being nurtured in other places, not in her original faith home. She finds beauty in the desert, in saguaro cacti, hummingbirds, the small and subtle and dry. This is where she is at home now.

Often members of our lesbian and bisexual community look at sexuality differently. It is something they don't take for granted. They find that they don't fit into the usual molds. They can question and *challenge gender roles,* and their differences allow them to move out of the boxes that many heterosexual women live in their whole lives. The lesbian women in our group are strong and independent, and they don't feel compelled to gain the attention of men. In relationships they negotiate about tasks around the house; in heterosexual relationships, society often dictates to a couple how they are to relate to each other and what roles they are to take on at home and socially. Our women live and promote *equality in relationships.*

As they help to shift and shake the assumptions and expectations relative to gender, they see themselves in a *prophetic role.* They have gifts to bring and perspectives to share with the wider community. Their sense of justice and equality is more acute because they have experienced prejudice and discrimination. Those who are out are taking a risk and are on the front lines of the social change that is happening in our country and world.

They develop skills and language for talking about their experience. They know that others cannot understand unless they first try to articulate what their experience has been. They find the *courage to tell the truth* in the face of, and in spite of, any adversity they might encounter because of it. Alice tells us in her story about the risk she took in coming out to her parents and the consequences she suffered because of that. And yet after a while she and her mother share a moment of grace.

Our women are motivated by a deep desire for their own freedom and a passion for justice not just for themselves and the women they love, but with a larger heart's yearning so that there is *freedom for everyone.* Many members of our community want a better life, not just for themselves, but for others, especially the younger generation, so they can feel better about themselves and have more job and housing, partnership and adoption rights in the future.

This spiritual journey enables them to come to an *integration of spirituality and sexuality.* They realize they are whole persons and that compartmentalizing their lives is not the way to go. They recognize the *holiness of the erotic* and that relationships are blessings.

This list is not complete or definitive; it represents the reflections of the twenty-one thoughtful, prayerful women who wrote for our project and have been able to work through many issues. They have come to attain a level of maturity, wisdom, and peace. Some remain in the church, and some do not. Yet all of them have made a significant contribution to the church and the people they have loved in it.

CELEBRATING

If you surrender to the air, you can ride it.

—*Toni Morrison*

Recollections...

Stories that Transform

About a year after our initial gathering, as our monthly meetings are coming to an end, I find myself musing about this writing project—one that has been neither smooth nor easy. I can feel both the pain and the joy of our writers and group members. I am nearly moved to tears when I realize the hurt, discrimination, and betrayal that these women have experienced. I am also moved to tears when I read about the joy they experience now because they can embrace themselves, their sexuality, and their faith.

This journey has been like finding faith through doubt and hope through despair. It has required taking a path that is mysterious and unknown. It has meant remembering times and places that have taken us where we may not have wanted to go. Our women may remain Catholic or find another spiritual home. I, along with them, live in a paradoxical place, feeling comfort and feeling angry at the same time. I realize how strong our women are, how committed, and how together they/we find a way.

I hear echoes from the stories at our meetings and when I read the stories, I hear resonances from the women in our group. Then I hear Mary Ann saying, "I come to this meeting because I see myself as a spiritual woman," and I am brought back to the present, sitting here in our group. I hear laughter; I hear the soft cadence of voices sharing deeply.

As I look around the room, I see each face. I notice the glow in each one. And I think about how transforming this process is for them. It brings new life to us in our circle. We are stronger together. What we experience here is truly sacred.

I see deep faith and compassion in abundance from our women, great gifts, given freely. I feel enveloped by the acceptance they offer to me and to one another.

I think again about the personal journeys that we have shared. I know that these separate journeys are really simply diverse ways that we express the One Universal Journey that we all travel.

Pride 2008

Ruth Mallery

Ruth is a country girl at heart, turned loose in the city. When not pursuing her passion for wandering around riverbanks fishing, she can be found blissfully becoming purposefully irrelevant. As president and founding member of the "Weird Club," her other hobbies include ladybug hunting, stone petting, and butterfly outfitting.

Pride was not one of the seven deadly sins this day. This day, it was a shorter word for "Rejoice, oh people of God, Alleluia!" Amanda found a solitary spot on a grassy portion of the sidewalk and sat down, waiting for the "Loud, Out, and Proud" beginning of Pride 2008. The smell of early morning grass, the sight of Dykes on Bikes—machine and majesty—the taste of a cold Budweiser, and the memory of Rachel permeated the suburban streets. It was the first time since Amanda had returned to the church that she had the nerve to go to the parade. It was a lonely kind of day, too, because Rachel was with someone else. It's not so much that she pined for the return of a lost love, but it was a poignant reminder that this parade, the first since God found her again, was something else that Amanda was doing alone.

Sometimes, alone is a good thing. A person needs to return to center and get grounded. After Rachel, a seventeen-year-long relationship that felt like lifetimes, Amanda had returned to the God that loved her better than any girlfriend ever did. After getting kicked out of the church by a homophobic priest; and after many side trips in and around various forms of Christianity, Native American spiritualism, Buddhism, and then nothing; finally nature, in all her majesty, soothed Amanda's soul. The Goddess and the God of Wicca comforted Amanda and helped her make sense of the world. She forgot that she had once been a child of the light. She forgot about being baptized priest, prophet, and royalty. She forgot that the Catholic Church had chewed her up and spit her out like worn-out gum. The rituals of Wicca did not remind her of the Christmas Crib; they did not remind her of the pain of missing Bread and Wine. She could pray to God and did not have to face the pain of what happened with her and the church, with her and Jesus. Wicca sufficed for joy and connection to the divine after Rachel. Wicca came after Rachel and before The Fire.

As Amanda waited for the parade to start, she chugged her beer and reached for the second one that was in her cooler. And she choked back tears. It had been a hot day, pretty much like this one, when Amanda had been driving around the city where she lived:

coming off the tail-end of her breakup; studying in a coven of intelligent, left-wing, lesbian feminist Pagans; and totally lost in a new city. The old car she was driving was falling apart, and before she knew what happened, she had to pull off the side of the road because black smoke and flames were coming out from under the hood of the car.

"Damn it. Not in front of a Catholic church."

The words that Amanda uttered to the poor friar who came out and asked her if she wanted help were even less reverent than that. He helped her put out the fire without saying much. When it was out, he offered to let her use his phone for the tow truck.

"You can wait in the church if you want. It's a hot day."

"Thanks, but I'd rather not."

"Suit yourself."

As the twenty-minute wait for the tow truck turned into two hours, and the outdoor temperature soared past one hundred degrees, Amanda wandered into the church. Memories flooded her brain, and her nose was full of the particular smell of Catholic incense and old candles. The German-style church was overwhelmingly beautiful. Statues of saints and angels were everywhere. It was dark and quiet, and there, over in the corner, was the Eucharist. Tentatively, Amanda walked through the church, flooded with nostalgia, anger, and even though she didn't know it, grace.

She had not been in a Catholic church since that priest told her she was a disgrace to God. She thought that the whole point of excommunication was to bring about conversion, but she could not be sorry for following her own conscience. She could not be sorry for who she *was*. The memory of his reaching past her to hand Communion to the people behind her in line was enough to make her turn toward the door.

Then the kids came in to practice for the school Mass. She hesitated just a minute.

In a way that brought her back to a time when she was fourteen years old and innocent, a child's girlish voice came over the microphone.

"The Lord is my shepherd. I shall not want."

Amanda froze.

"…he leads me beside still waters, and restores my soul…."

Tears were streaming down her cheeks as the child finished the psalm.

"…and I will dwell in the house of the Lord forever."

Angry that she had let herself be moved by the Living Word, Amanda dismissed her tears.

"That's all very quaint, but this place doesn't want me here. I am a disgrace to their so-called God." Amanda covered her tears behind a wall of anger. Where was that tow truck anyway? Hastily, she turned toward the door. She had been in the church just long enough to be slammed with exactly enough grace to get her to the next step. On the back of the door, in a prominent place, there was a sign hanging at eye level.

"Safe and affirming, Journey for Life, Gay Lesbian Bisexual Transgender Catholic Retreat. Call the parish office or John for more details." She also happened to have a pen in her pocket. Just exactly enough grace. Because if she walked out without getting John's number, she would have talked herself out of coming back.

Little did she know that she would be drenched in grace and roses from God for the next two years as she found the courage and strength to come back. Amanda wanted God. And apparently, God wanted Amanda.

Amanda's reverie shifted slightly as the parade marched past her. As the floats and marchers paraded past, she recalled years and years of struggle and loss during the AIDS outbreak. She recalled political efforts from Lifting the Ban and campaigning to overturn sodomy laws in the South. She remembered the funerals. The rush to the bank before the death certificate was issued to get money for the partner to have food before the estranged family showed up to claim "their child." She remembered the deception of renting a two-bedroom apartment as roommates, since it was illegal to rent a one bedroom to same-sex couples. She recalled the people who had helped her and Rachel wade their way through a somewhat homophobic foster-care system. She remembered bashing the church. She remembered rejecting their idea of God. The God Amanda understood knew that love was not wrong. She remembered the letter stuffing for political campaigns, the rallies, the wild parties, and the even still wilder parties. She remembered the egg that was thrown on her Halloween costume in the Castro. She remembered not caring because of the absolute joy of being in love. She remembered Rachel's very last kiss. And then once again she remembered The Fire.

"Lift up your hearts."

"We lift them up to the Lord."

She was so full of gratitude. She could not forget that even this parade was an extension of the Mass, a mission of our lived experience as another Christ in the world. It had been a long hard road back. Forgiveness does not come easy. And asking forgiveness was tough too. Sure that priest bashed her. And her family situation was…complicated. And she returned the favor by reacting with anger and hateful words towards anything remotely Catholic. And there was starting over again, after the breakup, and again when her Wicca Friends did not want her to get hurt again by "those damn Catholics." It was hard to be almost forty and start over, twice. And on top of that, more death, and sickness.

But when God gives roses, it is a humbling experience. She recalled another priest, in that church with the poster and the statues of saints and angels, who apologized for the priest who wouldn't. She teared up when she thought of still another one who told her to go to Communion. No questions asked. She needed him to be that direct. And after twenty-six years, six months and four days, she was filled with the source of life and hope and peace. And she had to swallow hard when this sister talked about the mercy—the loving kindness of God—without even mentioning the word sin. Just be willing to put oneself in a place where God can work. And God worked.

And it was gratitude and pain that let her be open to reconciliation. Not confession of fault, at first, and not apologizing for her person, but later on, apologizing for her bashing. And learning to be accepting of welcome, hospitality, and love. This was a dance of balancing, harmonizing, unifying. People at the church welcomed her. Almost to a person. She looked for reasons to leave. And they stayed. And they waited while she looked, and they ran after her when she got scared and ran away. And Amanda tried. And they tried. They broke bread. She longed for the chance simply to have Bread and Wine, but she was greeted with a Eucharist of inclusion, welcome and love. She volunteered. She looked for reasons to leave. She cried. She laughed. She loved and was loved. A child of the light. Precious.

In spite of herself, Amanda had come home. In the course of a year, she had reaffirmed her faith, joined several ministries, continued the letter writing and left-wing advocacy, and started to make peace with herself, the church and God.

"God hates fags!" "Repent. Jesus saves!"

Back at the parade, the people with crucifixes and large signs were up in her face, jolting her back to reality. She knew them. She was one of them. Hate in any form is not a stranger to any person. And she was another Christ. And this was an extension of the Mass.

Suddenly, after waiting her whole life, Amanda knew where she belonged. She knew where she was loved for who she was, as an entire person. And it wasn't at the wild parties that wound up bashing Christians. She was one of them too.

"Go out into the world and proclaim the good news!"

Her faith family would be there for her, even if these people beat her up. And the loud cacophony of zealots was getting more adamant and closer to her. Sometimes being alone was not such a great idea. At any rate, she raised her hands and began to pray a blessing over the protesters. They were other Christs too. This journey back to the church taught her to love your enemies and pray for those who hurt you. She was surprised at how natural it came.

Fortunately, about that time, the crowd of spectators had come over and noticed what was going on. And from the voices of her GLBT family, it seemed like a hundred lesbian and gay men's voices picked up the familiar tune, drowning out the sound of the hate.

"Jesus loves me, this I know, for the Bible tells me so." It was a weird song to sing at a gay pride parade, and it totally fit.

After a few minutes, the protestors noticed the police coming by and dissipated. Cheers erupted through the crowd. Right about that time the church groups and faith organizations paraded through. People from the coven Amanda had belonged to were coming down the street. She had had enough. It was time to go home.

After a quick change into a lavender dress, she was ready for choir practice. And before she even had time to blink, it was time for Communion. Looking around, she worshiped with other Christians she had seen at the parade. And still others that totally knew, and did not care, where they had been. It all came down to a simple, yet mysterious truth.

"The Body of Christ."

"Amen."

"The Blood of Christ."

In the silence that followed, Amanda was once again flooded with nostalgia and tears. Tears of gratitude. Being alone was of little significance that day. Amanda was fully alive. She finally was able to stand in front of God—in the church, with the Body of Christ—exactly as she was.

"I came that you might have life," says the Lord. "Life to the full."

My Butterfly Tattoo

Sylvia Squires

Sylvia was born in Chicago, Illinois, on April 27, 1942. She believes she could easily write a long book (and maybe she will) about the years between that day and her seventieth birthday, which she celebrated last April. Her life has been rich and full: sometimes very difficult, but always imbued with a faith that has been her rock and foundation. She is not religious; she is spiritual, and her continuing journey to wholeness and healing follows many paths.

Driving home from church recently, I stopped at a red light. I heard a voice from the car next to me saying, "I really like your tattoo." I looked over and saw a young black man and a young black woman smiling at me. I said, "Thank you," and the woman asked, "When did you get it?" I shouted back as the light changed, "Three years ago!" The young man smiled even bigger and gave me a signal with his right hand that clearly said, "You go, girl."

That gesture brought me back three years, to my "coming out." I didn't know at the time that that was what I was doing. My goddaughter had been trying to persuade me to get a tattoo for two years, and I kept saying, "I can't do that! I'm a religion teacher, I'm a lector, I'm a communion minister, I'm..."

Well, you get the point. Sixty-four-year-old women don't get tattoos.

This one did. I decided, without being fully aware of my own motivation, that I did want to get a tattoo. At the time my husband was in a nursing home receiving hospice care. I decided to take a day off from going to take care of him to go with my goddaughter to the Iron Age Tattoo Parlor.

As I was saying good-bye to my husband the day before, he asked about my plans for the following day. I replied that I was going to do something I had never done before. He immediately said, "You're going to get a tattoo." That left me speechless—as far as I knew, after almost twenty-eight years of marriage, he didn't even know my favorite color. I asked him how he knew, and he said, "It's simple. It's you. And I know what kind of tattoo you're going to get."

Now that was really too much. But he did know: "You're going to get a butterfly." The only part he got wrong was that he guessed I'd get it on my butt. "No way," I said. "I'm not going through all that pain to have a tattoo where no one, including me, can see it."

So for three years I've had a very colorful tattoo on the left side of my neck. I have realized that what I was really doing was making a statement about the future, and about who I was and who I intended to be. For all my life up to that day, I'd pretty much lived by what I thought people expected of me. From the day I got the tattoo, I discovered that a lot of people knew me far better that I knew myself. They weren't surprised or shocked. I asked some friends about that, and they all told me that this was not really out of character for me, and therefore was easily accepted as simply me being myself.

My husband died exactly one month after I got my tattoo. I had been in therapy for about two years, and during that time had "discovered" that I am a lesbian. I know that I had realized that many years before, but stuffing feelings and memories was something of a specialty of mine. The stress of taking care of my husband during a long and difficult illness wore me down emotionally, mentally, physically, and spiritually to the point where I simply didn't have the energy to keep all those feelings, memories, and realities stuffed down any more.

I came out to myself, but I had no idea what I would do after my husband died. Recognizing a truth and living it are very different things. I knew that I was not going to continue hiding from myself and other people, including my faith community—nor did I intend to go elsewhere and start over as a new person.

I was amazed that the family and friends I came out to were almost one hundred percent accepting. The people at my parish, which I had been a part of as Mrs. Daniel Squires for more than twenty-five years, did not hesitate in accepting this "new" me, this lesbian me. I'm only half teasing when I say that the relationship I have with my partner—a relationship of deep love and commitment—is legitimate because we met at church! I truly believe that our relationship is a gift from God, so I also believe that there is no one who has the right to judge or condemn our relationship, or us, and that includes bishops, cardinals, and the pope. I don't have any problem with sitting next to my partner/lover/friend and singing praise to God in God's house, because it's my house too—it's OUR house.

The butterfly on my neck symbolizes transformation, new life, freedom of the spirit. I am proclaiming that and claiming it as my right as a child of God—a much-favored child of God. Actually, we're all much favored, we LGBT Catholics, because God has given us the mission to open the minds and hearts and spirits of the leaders of the church to the beauty and diversity of God's children.

Catholic to the Core: On Refusing to Leave Home

Sheila Nelson

Sheila is a strange hybrid—part mystic, part social reformer. She loves music, poetry, small children, good novels, her college students, her cat Sibyl, and quilting. She also loves nature, sitting still, and being amazed at beauty and goodness. She is a sociologist who views her subject as a tool to transform the world—and maybe even the Catholic Church! She is an eternal optimist with an undying faith that the Spirit of God IS alive and at work in us.

I am a lesbian—and I am a Catholic…deeply, relentlessly, for better or for worse, hopelessly Catholic. It's in my blood, in my bones, at the core of my gut, in the very synapses of my brain, in both my conscious and my unconscious mind, in the center of my heart, in truly every fiber of my being. Oh, I've thought about leaving. Friends repeatedly ask me, "Why do you stay?" Or they invite me to join their churches: "You'd love our woman minister. She's great!" I sometimes reply, "Heck, if I joined your church I'd *become* the woman minister." When I joined my current parish and expressed a desire to get involved as a volunteer, I was given a vocation assessment tool to see what kind of ministry most suited my interests and gifts: it was a nondenominational instrument and not concerned with the Catholic distinction between men's roles and women's roles in the church. When I met a few days later with our parish volunteer coordinator (a woman, of course), we had a good laugh about the results: I would make a great pastor! Oh, I've thought about changing churches, but it's no use. I am who I am. And just as *lesbian* is at the core of my identity, so, too, is *Catholic.*

I was born and baptized into the Catholic community, and as difficult as the hierarchy makes it, I've got news for them—I'm not going anywhere. This is my home—and I'm not leaving! If those sound like fighting words, be forewarned. It's 2009 and I'm ready to fight. Or maybe not; maybe I'll heap fiery coals of love on those in power, and they'll have their eyes opened and repent of their narrowness. Or maybe I'll simply keep living here in my church home, worshiping and sharing faith and serving where I can, speaking my truth, refusing to hide in closets or run away, doing acts of faith and justice, and trusting in God's ever-present invincible Spirit.

How can I explain this strong sense of Catholic identity, this unwavering knowledge that I *belong* here? As a sociologist, I recognize that my family background and early socialization had much to do with it, though strangely enough, none of my siblings feels quite as strong a commitment to the Catholic Church as I. Our childhood home was filled with sacramentals: Jesus the Good Shepherd, Our Lady of Perpetual Help, Nativity scenes and Last Suppers, statues of the boy Jesus and of Mary, blessed candles, and May altars. Those early images of God were of a tender, compassionate, and loving God—one who knew me and saw me as *good*. We prayed before and after every meal, were blessed by our parents with holy water before bed, and recited the daily radio rosary every evening at 6:15. We went to Catholic school, as had my mother and her parents before her. The culture was thoroughly Catholic—Catholic Girl Scout troop, Catholic Daughters, daily Mass...all the kids in the neighborhood were Catholic.

I was probably in third grade when my little Catholic girl idealism got a strong boost. I was enamored with Sister Mary, my teacher, and my best friend was Joey. Joey was in our boys' choir and sang like an angel. The two of us skipped home from school each day holding hands, often with Joey singing to me. We didn't think there was anything unusual about the life plan we were hatching together. Looking back now at those sweet memories, I smile, understanding what I couldn't have possibly imagined at the time. Our plan: after eighth grade I would enter the convent, and Joey would enter the seminary. He'd become a priest and I a nun, and then we would be stationed in the same parish, serve God together, and be best friends forever. Well, we carried out the first part of the dream. At age fourteen I entered the convent and Joey the seminary, but then we lost touch with each other. At that point, I had no idea I was a lesbian—I didn't know what that meant. And it was forty some years later that I discovered that Joey was gay. Somehow, way back then, we were drawn together in our differentness—and interpreted it in the only way we knew: "we must be called to the religious life."

Something else also began developing in me in the third grade. That was the year John Kennedy was elected the first Catholic president of the United States. There was such enormous pride in the Catholic community. My dad gave my sister and me donkey pins with "KENNEDY" written across the bottom—I still have that pin today. And my first memory of political involvement was my third-grade class—all fifty of us and Sister Mary—singing "Jack is on the right track" to the tune of *High Hopes*. Kennedy was wildly popular, and he engendered such pride and optimism and willingness to serve—a belief that we could build a better world. Catholicism and patriotism really went together during the 1960s!

The significance of this historical event was reinforced when John XXIII was elected Pope. An older man, he quickly won the respect of the whole world when he wrote the powerful encyclical *Pacem In Terris* (Peace on Earth) and attempted to make Catholicism more open and responsive to the rest of the world. It was John XXIII who convened the Second Vatican Council—a council that challenged Catholics to care deeply about the poor and those most marginalized in society. When my parents bought a home when I was in sixth grade, it was the Pope's picture that I hung on my new bedroom wall! Kennedy, by initiating programs like the Peace Corps, and John XXIII stirred up the idealism in my young heart—and early on I felt called to a life of service, to somehow spend my life fighting the inequality that was so prevalent in our society. I came to view Catholicism as providing a powerful challenge to injustice and inequality. It was vibrantly clear to me, in those years of church reform, that the Catholic Church called me to do something about every social reality that keeps people down, prevents them from living in dignity and reaching their full potential. How unfortunate that this church that taught me to see and respond to the needs of the oppressed now attempts to silence and alienate me! Who are the poor and marginalized? Are not gays, lesbians, and transgendered persons in need of a voice and human dignity?

My entering the convent after grade school is not at all surprising. Living in Sheboygan, Wisconsin, I had no exposure to gays or lesbians, no understanding of sexual orientation. I needed someone to reflect back to me who I was—but there was no one. I knew deep down somehow that I was different, but it was a difference I couldn't name and didn't know how to interpret. So, based on my Catholic culture, it makes sense that I believed I was being called to religious life. I was attracted to the sisters who taught me in school—lots of young, vibrant, intelligent women—and they looked so beautiful in their flowing black habits! I knew I didn't want to get married, and this was a choice that brought me lots of positive feedback. Of course the sisters were happy to see that I was interested in joining the convent; my grandmother, whom I adored, confided that she had once wanted to be a nun. My parents were supportive, though they didn't want me to leave home that young. All in all, rather than being ridiculed and stigmatized for being a lesbian, I was held in high esteem for my desire to be a sister. I don't regret those years in the convent. They provided me with a strong spirituality, deep prayer life, and good theology; they taught me to trust God within me—and to understand the concept of freedom of conscience. This strong grounding in religious life has been key in my ability to stay within the Catholic institution while embracing my sexual orientation.

I loved religious life—the community, the ritual, the rhythm of work and prayer and friendship. The late '60s and early '70s was a wonderful time to be a sister. Vatican II's call to renewal was taken seriously: in formation, we studied the council documents as well as the constitution of the congregation—which had just been updated. The formal prayers of the Divine Office were supplemented with "faith sharing," reflections on how God was at work in our personal lives. We explored various forms of spirituality. We were given graduate training in theology—and there was no fear of "liberation theology," which so stimulated my spirit and nourished my heart.

The call that was confirmed in us was a call to engage our world rather than to withdraw from it; and while we were still prepared for the traditional work of the congregation, teaching and nursing, we young sisters were encouraged to participate in volunteer work during the summer that sensitized us to what the institutional church was calling the "preferential option for the poor." I spent four summers working for a Methodist Community Center's program for low-income black children in Mobile, Alabama. Friends in Community worked in Harlem, in rural Oregon, and with Hispanics in New Mexico. In each of these settings we worked side by side with dedicated people, usually just a little older than we, who had committed their lives to building a more just and equitable world, and who proved to be marvelous mentors. They patiently answered our questions, opened our eyes to the bigger reality, and guided us out of the protective bubble that our Midwestern backgrounds and convent training had unwittingly created. The women with whom I worked in Mobile shared their experiences with the civil rights movement and Dr. Martin Luther King, Jr. They taught us about the structural disadvantages facing the kids; they showed us the neighborhoods and how city and state governments had isolated the poor; they talked about the prison system and the injustices inherent there.

We worked an eight-hour day in the school, but most nights one of our mentors would appear at the parish house we were given for the summer, and debrief with us, laugh with us, inspire us. We received so much from those experiences—tasting a little bit of freedom from the structure of religious life, but much more importantly, coming to know what life was like for so many people in our country who lacked the basics that we had taken so much for granted. It was through these summer experiences that I learned a couple of essential lessons: 1) not all committed people lived in convents, rectories, and monasteries—there were wonderful people who dedicated their lives to justice and promoting cultural understanding; 2) differences were enriching—if I had been working for middle-class white women, no matter how good and talented they were, I wouldn't have learned nearly as much as I did from those who shared the pains, struggles, and richness of their own racial, geographic, and class background—who enabled me to see things from another perspective, while affirming that human core, that spirit common to us all. It was also through these experiences that I discerned the call to leave elementary teaching and to study first social work and then sociology.

But while all this positive development was going on, I was also being rewarded for living from my neck up—staying in my head and distrusting emotions. We laughed at obsolete notions like "particular friendships," which had until recently protected sisters from inappropriate relationships by greatly restricting the time one could spend with any other. These rules about not walking with the same sister during recreation two nights in a row, or not writing to individual sisters once you had been transferred to another ministerial setting, were no longer enforced. But the "good sister" loved everyone, sexuality was certainly suppressed, and passion—or even attraction—was something to be feared and regarded with suspicion. We were to be above all that—and, unfortunately, many of us were, as we lived outside of our bodies. For me this meant that I did not come to understand and accept my sexual orientation until I was in my late thirties.

One summer when I was studying graduate theology in a program whose students were primarily nuns, one of my friends took a course on sexuality. Every night all of us on her floor in the dorm gathered around to hear a recap of that day's class. Obviously we were all curious and eager for information. One night, she shared a test that supposedly measured where a person was on the continuum of sexual orientation. Most of us were afraid to actually answer the questions, and we consoled ourselves with the thought that the test wouldn't be accurate for us who lived in convents and had had very limited opportunities to interact with men. But it started me wondering—what did my fantasies mean? Was I a lesbian? I considered the question for a couple of weeks, but concluded that it was irrelevant, since I was a celibate. Once again I escaped to my head and shut down my body. But there was a growing hunger inside me that I couldn't quite ignore. It haunted me and returned persistently during my last year of elementary school teaching. I didn't know what it meant, but as uncomfortable as the hunger was, it seemed to be of God, a grace being offered to me.

At age thirty-one my life began to change. I left for graduate school—full time—far away from the rest of my community. While I lived in a residence hall for religious women, for the first time I was without the sisters who had directed my life from first grade on. It was a time of growing up—I had to make my own friends, create my own schedule, decide my own priorities, build the community that I wanted...all things I had never done before. It was a very freeing experience—and I delighted in the sense of being responsible for myself. For the first time, I felt responsible for my own life—setting expectations for myself rather than responding to the expectations of others. Here was a safe environment where I could confront that persistent hunger and try to discover what it meant. In that atmosphere of freedom and safety, of familiarity and difference, it's not surprising that dramatic change happened at a whirlwind pace. Within the first month, I had fallen in love. I didn't admit it yet, and I certainly didn't know what it would come to mean or how dramatically it would change my life, but it happened, and I was enjoying it—secretively, pretending it was just a growing friendship, but deep inside a strange new knowledge was beginning to develop and undiscovered parts of me were awaking and silently screaming for attention.

I didn't dive right into the experience of love and romance. Instead, I hid my feelings, disguised my love, refused to speak of what was becoming increasingly difficult to deny. True to all my training, I suppressed my hunger, tried to tame my passion, and confined my love within the bounds of my commitment to religious life and celibacy. Literally, it took years before I confronted my situation head-on. When I finally did, there followed a period that I remember fondly as my Garden of Eden—experiencing the sheer joy of life and love, tasting the fruit of trees God gives us for our enjoyment and nourishment, discovering with my beloved a whole new world and reality, feeling enormously blessed and gifted, and delighting in that knowledge. It was a time of innocence, of contentment, of experiencing life as I truly believe God intended it to be lived by us. The call was powerful: "Accept the gifts I give you! Embrace all of who you are and *celebrate* it—for that is where you will find me!" The self-denial that had been so honored during earlier years now seemed wrong. If God made me to be me, if I was created in God's image, if God's creation is *good,* why should I deny myself? Wasn't that denying God, denying God's creation, and God's gift? Sacrifice for the sake of sacrifice was gradually losing its meaning. Sacrifice was still necessary—but it was sacrifice in order to grow, to develop into the woman I was meant to be…and sacrifice that would help create a world where all people could do the same.

I could not have made this journey into the Garden of Eden and on into lesbian adulthood if it hadn't been for wonderful women of spirit who listened compassionately to me, provided me with direction and support, taught me to confront my fears and to laugh at myself, and encouraged me to trust the God within. Rather than shutting me down and warning me of the dangerous territory I was exploring, they encouraged me to put out into the deep water and discover who I was and what would give me life. I will never forget my spiritual director saying to me during a directed retreat, "When you're okay with who you are, it won't matter what the bishops say or what statements Rome makes." She encouraged me to integrate mind, heart, and gut—to listen to my longings and to see them as God's revelation.

Once I embraced myself as a lesbian, I had to deal with the question of whether to stay in religious life or to move on, freed from the vows I had made before I understood who I was. Having always felt "called," having had beautiful experiences of community, loving my sisters in religious life, being committed to the mission and charism of my congregation, having found community life enriching and happy, the thought of leaving was frightening—and confusing. For years I felt caught on the fence, wanting somehow to integrate the two realities, the two calls I felt—to committed love of another woman and to committed love for a religious congregation. Sharing my dilemma with a therapist, with my congregation's leadership, with other lesbian nuns, with my friends in community, were important steps, but I remained stuck.

Finally I did a mask-making retreat with an artist friend of mine. As I created the mask of the strong woman I wanted to be, of the woman not bound by convention or by the expectations others had of her, my artist guide encouraged me to pay close attention to my dreams. About two days into the retreat, I had a dream that I truly believe was God's intervention, rescuing me from my struggle. I dreamt I was walking along a riverbank when I heard a baby crying. I hurried down the bank to the river, where I found a small baby tightly wrapped in a plastic bag. I scooped up the baby, and just as I was about to tear open the bag, I suddenly stopped and heard myself saying, "But the baby is breathing. It is able to survive in this bag." With that I woke up and knew immediately that I was the baby and the bag was religious life. I knew now with certainty that I could remain in religious life and I'd survive, but I wouldn't be living a full and free life. I'd be surviving but not living. That dream gave me the courage to take leave of my sisters and strike out on my own—with a deeply renewed sense of personal integrity.

I was fortunate to have a congregation that supported me, that was willing to let go of me, to release me from my commitment to them with blessings and forgiveness. And since then I look back fondly on my years in community and recognize how central they have been to my personal and spiritual development. I needed to leave home to become the woman that I am, but I will forever be grateful for the grounding and wisdom I was given in both my family home and my congregational home. My love for the Catholic Church, my willingness to actively work within the church for inclusion, is in great part possible because of all that I was given, and the woman that I became in religious community.

My transition to being a lay Catholic went smoothly. For me, it was a real relief to be myself, to no longer have to represent the institutional church as others had expected of me as a Catholic sister. As many young people do when they want to come out of the closet, I moved far away from home to a place where no one knew me and I could start over, forging a new identity. I am fortunate to be a sociologist and to have found a professional home for myself on a Catholic campus—where the Benedictine monks and monastic women are open, inclusive, and wonderfully supportive of me and responsive to the needs of GLBT persons. I see the job here as one of God's gifts of love for me as I transitioned. While interviewing for this position, I was invited to dinner in the sisters' dining room and was seated at a table with several college teachers and some retired sisters. During dinner, conversation switched to the woman for whose position I was interviewing, a woman who had died of cancer at a very young age the previous year. One of the sisters casually commented to the others, "We really must do something for her partner. She moved here for Janet, and now since Janet's death she has been left all alone. We really must reach out to her and see how she is doing!" I'm sure my mouth dropped as it sank in that they were speaking in such a compassionate and affirming way of a committed lesbian relationship. Here was a place where I could be whole—affirming both my faith identity and my sexual orientation. It was clear that God had prepared a safe place for me, and I have never regretted this move. Here I am able to be open and out in the classroom as well as with my colleagues. I have built a research agenda around GLBT issues and the challenge of integrating religion and sexual orientation. My work with GLBT faculty and staff and with GLBT students is affirmed and valued. I have found a life-giving community that has become home.

But even that probably wouldn't have been enough to keep me in the institutional church. The Catholic Church continues to be a home for me because of the many people—the Body of Christ—who live the Gospel of love and inclusion. We don't always agree—and there are many in my parish family who do not know that I am a lesbian—and wouldn't understand if they knew; but every family has its disagreements, its clashes, its inability to see eye to eye on certain issues. That is simply the reality of our human condition and of living in a less than perfect world. But there are many others in my parish family who *do* know and love me for who I am, who see me as part of the family, as one of them rather than as someone special or especially burdened or in need of special prayers or healing. I have found pastors who are truly pastoral, who listen with their hearts, who care rather than judge. I have read and heard Catholic theologians reflect on the reality of homosexuality and see it as a gift of diversity for the church rather than as a problem. I have cried tears of joy and hope when they have spoken words of wisdom, often at great personal cost, when they have risked speaking truth to power on my behalf. I have found wonderful, brilliant, dedicated companions on my journey, people who care as deeply as I do for this struggling church of ours. Working together, we *can* and *will* make a difference, *will* build a more inclusive church, *will* become progressively more and more the *people of God* that Christ envisioned, died to bring into being, and continues to call us to be.

In practical terms, this means being involved in promoting understanding at the local level in whatever way I can. It also means working through organizations committed to similar goals. The Catholic Association of Lesbian and Gay Ministry (formerly NACDLGM) is one such organization. The annual conferences of this group bring together from around the world priests, religious, lay ministers, GLBT Catholics, and the Catholic parents of GLBT persons. We share stories; share faith; pray together; and learn from current research in theology, pastoral ministry, and the social sciences how to make room at the table for our GLBT brothers and sisters. For me, each gathering is a celebration of who I am, of who we are, and of what the church is called to be and is, by our efforts, becoming! Every September I receive this powerful injection—of pride and promise and hope. I come away with renewed energy to keep believing, to keep sharing my story and searching for the Truth within me, to stay with this church which is so much more than pope and bishops and laws and pronouncements. Being with this group keeps me grounded and focused on what is essential—and what is essential is why I stay.

The Catholic Church is my home; it is here that I am nourished each day. It is the foundation upon which all my other identities are built, and which integrates my life and gives a sense of purpose to all the varied pieces of my life. Whether it is a powerful liturgy, an especially moving song, the inspiration of one of those simple and authentic people who simply glows with Christ-light, a particularly striking line from scripture, a reflection that colors how I view my day, or any of the other myriad graces that daily give my life meaning, so much of my spirit life comes to me via Catholicism. I cannot imagine how empty my life would be without these touches of the Divine—and without being able to celebrate and share them regularly with a faith community. Yes, we're a motley group, and sometimes we don't even like each other very much, but isn't that part of the Catholic "good news"? Central to Catholic belief is the conviction that human life is sacred, that all persons are made in God's image, have dignity, belong. There is room for everyone, holding hands around the altar and praying together despite our differences. We proclaim a God big enough to embrace and forgive *all* of us! It's a beautiful vision and one I continue to build my life on.

So, no, I'm not leaving my church. I certainly understand my brothers and sisters who need to go because of the intensity of the hurt, the reality of the abuse, the absence of the nourishment they so desperately need. But I feel God's call to stay right where I am, to sink my roots ever deeper, to renew my commitment daily. I stay for myself, but I also stay for the children. I stay to create a safe place in my church for them, for all those future generations of GLBT persons who will love the sacramental life and worldview of the Catholic Church as much as I do. And I stay for the sake of this church that I love— because my church *needs* those children, needs their vision and their gifts, needs— perhaps most—the very ones some would try to drive away. I envision a day in the not-too-far-distant future, when no one will feel forced to leave: no one will leave because they don't feel they have any other option. I imagine that many will still choose to leave, but I want it to be their free choice rather than an experience of such alienation that they feel driven away from their home. I work for that day. I have lived long enough to recognize the truth of the mystery: God is in the struggle; God is in the hunger; God is in the agony and the ecstasy of our striving to be authentically who we are. As for me, this is where I am finding my God. This is who I am. How could I ever go anywhere else?

Reflections...

Freedom of Integrity

As we invite women to write about being Lesbian/Bisexual and Catholic, we look at both these terms in the broadest sense. Being Catholic means having been raised Catholic and most of the women have been baptized as babies. It also included becoming Catholic at any time in one's life; some of our women, like Sylvia, are "converts" to Catholicism.

Some members of our writing group have been Catholic but find that the only way they can embrace themselves fully is to no longer be called Catholic. Yet, often even for them, there is a longing to be Catholic. Some of them become members of other churches or stop going all together, but still there is a Catholic core somewhere in their being. Amanda leaves the church, and after some time finds herself back and feeling at home again.

We talk about being Catholic. Who is Catholic? Who speaks for the church? What makes us Catholic?

Something that speaks deeply to me is that we baptize infants. It is such an affirmation of God's love for us and of the church at its best, embracing all of us. We simply become Catholic. We don't have to be worthy, to take a test or prove ourselves in any way.

The earliest church experience was that of baptism of adults: being Catholic was a conscious choice. Of course, I am talking about a very early church, which was when we were simply called Christian. When we baptize adults, we can make rules about who is worthy or entitled to belong to our church. We do this with our Rite of Christian Initiation of Adult program, give people a spiritual experience, and accompany them on a journey to becoming Catholic.

But our tradition is strong to presume worthiness or at least to believe that any unworthiness we have is washed away in our baptism. We put on Christ and become Christ and our very bodies are temples of the Spirit, regardless or who we are or who we will become. Of course, the church community, beginning with our parents, speaks for us declaring desires we cannot yet name, promising to walk this journey with us so that we can grow into mature and believing Christian/Catholics.

I myself have a strong sense of being Catholic. It is in the fiber of my being, my core identity. I cannot not be Catholic. I grew up surrounded by a Catholic culture, a house filled with religious artifacts. I went to a Catholic school and all my friends and relatives were Catholic. I lived in a totally Catholic environment. Sheila writes about being Catholic in this same way, being "deeply, relentlessly, hopelessly" Catholic.

In these writings and in Jane and Joan's living room, we are church together and we support each other in our spiritual paths.

Afterword

The Still Silent Voices

Four and a half years, and one thousand eight hundred and fourteen e-mails later, here I am writing a conclusion to our book. We contacted forty local women at the beginning of this project. Then after ten or twelve months, we e-mailed seven organizations that got the word out for us. We received forty-six responses. We have these twenty-one stories to share with you. These stories represent the voices of women who have resolved some questions and who are able to embrace themselves.

What happened to the rest of the sixty some writers? These are the women who could not, would not, or did not write.

Fear silences many. Some are just too tired to deal with this issue yet again. Some are depressed. Some are still angry. For some, writing is a challenge they prefer not to take up. Some just want to keep their stories to themselves.

Whatever the case, there are more stories out there. Many of the women I have talked to and who showed early interest and enthusiasm about the project are still silent.

One woman, who was a part of this project for a while, sent me an e-mail about going to the New York legislature to lobby for the state equality in marriage act. This is what she wrote of her experience, "There are no words that describe the hate we felt. Twice I broke down crying because I could not believe the anger and negativity from the ministers and congregation members present. I think I finally know what it feels like to be rejected, hated, and treated as evil and perverse. 'You are going to hell. You are freaks. You are sinners,' they shouted at us. I cry every time I think about it."

Actions like this contribute to the silence.

Another woman I know did not fully realize her orientation until she was more than sixty years old. Her husband was dying and a nurse held her to comfort her. She experienced a physical reaction to the nurse that startled her. Shortly after that, she met a woman in church on Holy Saturday just after her husband had died. She fell in love with her. At sixty something she said, "Now I know who I am."

I know women who are attracted to women and suppress their feelings. One in particular stands out in my mind, a woman I know who does not let herself realize her identity. A number of my friends believe her to be lesbian. Yet she has lived more than fifty years without allowing herself to access the creative energy of her sexuality. I feel sad for her, being deprived of an essential part of who she is.

I know other women who are simply confused. They might date women and then back away from the lesbian community. Some even begin dating men again. Others don't date men, but hide behind pretending to be attracted to them.

But those who have written here have found healing and a sense of pride in being able to claim their identity.

The experiences still go on. More and more stories are being lived out. Let us allow our sisters to speak up. Let us invite them to come out.

Appendix

Welcoming Our Sisters

Now that you have read the stories and met some incredible women, I would like to suggest some things that you can do to be more supportive of our lesbian, bisexual, and transgendered sisters. These are ideas that have come from members of our community, from discussions we have had, from suggestions individuals and groups have made, from complaints about how unwelcoming some parishes are, from some deep longings and wishes that "I can recognize myself when I come to church here. When I see other members of my community, I feel welcomed. When I see gays and lesbians take an active part in the liturgy, I feel welcomed. When I hear references to people like me in the prayers and homilies, I feel like I belong."

Personal Actions

Personally you can simply reach out more. Be more inviting at church when you see some-one new. Just exude more warmth in general. It will be good for everyone, even yourself. You do not have to go out and try to find lesbian and bisexual women; they may already be sitting right next to you. You probably already know a few who are not out to you yet.

Have an open attitude. Bring up the subject. Claim your advocacy. Tell others you are concerned about members of the LGBT community. If you mention this to a straight person, you are still spreading welcome and equality. It may make the woman you are speaking to think about reaching out more as well. If someone is offended, don't let that stop you. You are an advocate. This is a justice issue. If you act as though it is normal to be lesbian or bisexual, it helps others to gain a new perspective as well.

When you know a woman who is lesbian, just be your already gracious self. Treat her like you treat others. If she is single, it is okay to ask her if she is dating someone. Show interest in the women in her life. Ask her if she has a partner. When you see a couple, talk to them.

Develop friendships with members of the LGBT community. Know about significant members of our community and their contributions to our society. Many influential historical figures were gay or lesbian. Bring them up in conversation. Talk about the accomplishments of lesbian athletes, actors, politicians, social workers, doctors, and lawyers.

Attend LGBT events. Go to a Pride Parade; visit the booths that are set up at your local PrideFest. Support gay and lesbian businesses.

With the help of the Internet you can ask your favorite search engine to find people and places so you can be supportive of the community. Many cities have Pride Pages that list gay-and-lesbian-friendly businesses and services.

Support LGBT efforts for justice. Organizations that work for equality can also be found on the Internet. Find a group whose values you share and become a member. Get their action alerts. Act on those you are comfortable supporting. Stand in solidarity with your sisters.

Invite your lesbian neighbor to go to church with you, if she is interested. When you know a lesbian woman at church, invite her to be involved, suggest her name for a committee. Invite her to have a role in the parish.

Getting Your Parish Involved

Create a welcoming environment for LGBT Catholics, their families, friends, and allies at your parish. Initiate a committee to plan and coordinate welcoming activities and act as host. Advertise your parish in gay publications and event programs. Think about this as an evangelization effort for your parish. Have welcoming fliers in the back of your church and publish bulletin announcements that tell others you are welcoming. Distribute information about your parish in gay districts. Give out a welcoming brochure to all new members that lets everyone know you are a welcoming faith community.

If you have already done the above and you want to be more involved, go to your local PrideFest. Distribute brochures inviting members of the LGBT community to your parish. Have a welcoming social. Engage in home visits to welcome everyone and let the lesbians and bisexual women know you welcome them, too. Go to neighborhood association meetings and let new members in your neighborhood know you are welcoming. Initiate interfaith prayer services that reach out to everyone and especially invite the LGBT community. Offer retreats or other spiritual events for the gay community.

Oppose discrimination and injustice by developing and enhancing parish communities of respect, compassion, and support. Publish bulletin announcements for significant LGBT days, like the anniversary of Matthew Shepard's death or World AIDS day. Offer prayers of the faithful for those who have died because of hate crimes. Host a prayer service to foster nonviolence and include LGBT violence in the prayer. Mention discrimination in homilies.

Promote healing and reconciliation in your parish. Have sessions for your parishioners about church teaching on sexual morality. Talk openly about what a healthy sexuality looks like. Encourage your parishioners to work for integration sexually and spiritually. Invite LGBT parents to come together for a support group. Have information sessions and resources for those who have been previously married to a gay or lesbian spouse.

Educate your parish community on issues and concerns of the gay and lesbian community. Let members of the LGBT community speak about their concerns. Use art, music, theatre, and movies to communicate the experience of being lesbian or gay.

Empower LGBT Catholics to share their gifts and talents with and for your parish. Invite members of the LGBT community to join small church communities or other discussion/support groups. Encourage LGBT members to volunteer for parish organizations and committees. Make sure our LGBT community is represented throughout the parish, on committees, commissions, and parish councils. Help members of our community develop leadership potential.

Many of these activities can be implemented easily. Some may require a team effort of committed parishioners who want to educate themselves and their parishioners and who want to take action to assure that their parish is a welcome and open faith community. Most of these actions are simply outreach activities that could be used to promote diversity with any minority group. Most are things we can all do to be more gracious and welcoming to the person in the pew next to us; after all that is who your LGBT members are.

List of Illustrations

About the Editors

Margaret O'Gorman, FSM

Marge is a Franciscan Sister of Mary serving her church as a spiritual director. She has spent most of her life as a pastoral minister in adult faith formation. She is committed to social justice and extends her compassion and advocacy efforts to care for our planet Earth. She is a seeker of God, rooted in scripture, prayer, and liturgy. She also experiences God as reflected in nature and in those on the margins of society.

Anne Peper Perkins

Anne received a PhD in Comparative Literature from Washington University in 1986 and taught Latin and Greek at Webster University for a number of years. She retired fifteen years ago in order to spend more time doing Healing Touch on cancer patients, teaching T'ai Chi Chih to children and adults, being very active in her church, and enjoying her six beautiful grandchildren. She has lived happily in St. Louis' Lafayette Square for nearly 25 years with her spouse Mary Sale.